GOOD·FOR·YOU
PASTA
COOKBOOK

OVER 125 DELICIOUSLY HEALTHFUL RECIPES

Linda Ferrari

PRIMA PUBLISHING

PRIMA PUBLISHING and its colophon, which consists of the letter P over PRIMA, are trademarks of Prima Communications, Inc.

Cover photography © Kent Lacin Media Services, Sacramento

Library of Congress Cataloging-in-Publication Data

Ferrara, Linda.
  Good-for-you pasta cookbook : over 125 deliciously healthful recipes / Linda Ferrari.
      p.   cm.
  Includes index.
  ISBN 0-76150124-x
  1. Cookery (Pasta)   I. Title.
TX809.M17F47   1995
841.8'22—dc20   94-32629
                                                                      CIP

95 96 97 DD 10 9 8 7 6 5 4

Printed in the United States of America

How to Order:
Single copies may be ordered from Prima Publishing, P.O. Box 1260, Rock-lin, CA 95677; telephone (916) 632-4400. Quantity discounts are also available. On your letterhead, include information concerning the intended use of the books and the number of books you wish to purchase.

Nutritional Analyses:
A per serving nutritional breakdown is provided for each recipe. If a range is given for an ingredient amount, the breakdown is based on the smaller number. If a range is given for servings, the breakdown is based on the larger number. If a choice of ingredients is given in an ingredient listing, the breakdown is calculated using the first choice. Nutritional content may vary depending on the specific brands or types of ingredients used. "Optional" ingredients or those for which no specific amount is stated are not include included in the breakdown. Nutritional figures are rounded to the nearest whole number.

CONTENTS

*To my mom and best friend, Evelyn Walker,
for always loving and encouraging me.*

Acknowledgments

Writing recipes is just the first step in the lengthy process of producing a cookbook. I am indebted to all who have helped me complete this book. Thank you to my publisher for having interest and continued support in this GOOD-FOR-YOU series. Thanks to Jennifer Basye Sander, Karen Blanco, and Andi Reese Brady at Prima and to Jane Gilligan for editing, Lindy Dunlavey for the cover, Neiel Cavin for interior illustrations, and Archetype Book Composition for layout.

I also want to acknowledge my cooking students, friends, and relatives who are all recipe testers. And a big thank you to my agent, Linda Hayes, for being there for me and to my friend Georgia Bockoven.

Introduction

Pasta is a universally loved food. It blends beautifully with many different flavors, providing an empty canvas for the inventive cook. A pasta dish can be made simple or complex—and taste delicious either way. I have reduced the fat in these recipes, yet have kept creativity and flavor alive. I promise that these dishes are not only rich and flavorful but also healthful.

When I was a child, my mother often made quick batches of homemade egg noodles and topped them with her spicy, homemade croutons right out of the oven. This may seem like a strange combination, but it was one of my favorite meals. Mom also rolled and cut out thin rounds of pasta that she dried on the kitchen table. She filled the pasta rounds with meat and rolled them up like crepes, then covered them with a superb sauce. Mom did this with such ease that making homemade pasta has never seemed a chore to me, but rather a pleasurable experience.

Homemade pasta is a delightful challenge. Making pasta dough by hand is simple, and after trying it a few times, you can become an expert. If you own a food processor, making pasta will become extremely fast and easy. For those who do not want to undertake making homemade pasta, you can revel in the variety of shapes, flavors, and colors of dried pastas available at supermarkets and gourmet shops.

Pasta cooks quickly, as do many of the sauces. Exciting and memorable meals may take only minutes to prepare. I hope you enjoy the recipes in this book and that many of them will become family favorites.

Following are my recommendations for equipment needed to make homemade pasta, a guide to the techniques used in making both pasta and stuffed pasta, a glossary describing different types of pastas, and a listing of the basic ingredients used in the recipes.

Equipment Needed

It takes very little equipment to make and cook pasta. All you need are a work surface (preferably wood), a fork, a rolling pin, a knife, a large pot, and a strainer (many pasta-cooking pots come with removable strainers).

A food processor to mix the dough and a manual pasta machine for rolling and cutting are very useful. Handy, but not essential, items include cookie and biscuit cutters to make various ravioli shapes, a fluted-edged pastry wheel to make ripple-edged lasagna noodles, a pastry bag with a large circle tip for filling stuffed pastas, a fettucini rolling pin, ravioli forms or a ravioli rolling pin, and a pasta drying rack.

Some cooks find electric pasta makers highly convenient. These machines merely require putting in flour and water, pushing a button, and waiting a few minutes for pasta to emerge. There are many different brands to choose from. I suggest viewing a demonstration of the machine you plan to purchase to see the quality of pasta produced and to see how easy it is to operate and to clean. If you find the right machine, it may turn you into an overnight gourmet chef.

Making Pasta Dough

If you make homemade pasta just once, any fears you have will disappear as you realize how easy it is. If you own a food processor, the process is even quicker and easier. Now, please take that processor out of the cupboard and use it. Many of my cooking class students confess to owning a machine but never using it. I leave my food processors out on the counter in easy reach. If I always had to pull them up and out of a cupboard, I probably would not use them either.

To make pasta dough in a food processor, insert the metal blade and place all the ingredients called for in the work bowl *except* for 1/2 cup of the flour. Process the ingredients, adding enough of the remaining 1/2 cup flour, 1 tablespoon at a time, until the dough is smooth and not sticky. Let the machine knead the dough for a couple minutes. Remove dough from the work bowl and shape into a ball on a floured work surface. Wrap the dough in plastic wrap and let rest for 20 minutes.

The traditional way of making pasta is by hand—a method I still take great pleasure in. Pour the flour (reserving 1/2 cup to add as necessary) into a mound on a floured work surface and make a well in the center of the mound. Crack the eggs into the well, then add the oil or water, salt, and optional flavoring. With a fork, carefully beat the liquid ingredients within the well, then gently incorporate the flour into the liquid as fast as you can. Begin kneading the dough by folding, pushing, and turning it, adding the reserved 1/2 cup of flour, 1 tablespoon at a time, until dough is smooth and not sticky. Shape dough into a ball and wrap in plastic wrap. Let rest for 20 minutes.

Rolling the Pasta Dough

Cut the dough into pieces the size of large apricots. Working one piece at a time, flatten the dough with your hand, then roll the pasta out from the center to the outer edge. Turn the dough around in a circle as you continue to roll from center to outer edge. Roll out the dough until it is about 1/8 inch thick. Continue rolling, if necessary, to get the desired shape and thickness.

If you have a manual pasta machine (my favorite piece of equipment), start with a piece of dough about the size of a large apricot. Set your machine on the highest numerical setting and crank the dough through the rollers. Fold this dough in thirds like a letter and pass through the machine two more times, folding in thirds each time. Make sure you sprinkle the dough with flour if it gets sticky. Continue to run pasta through the machine, no longer folding, lowering the numerical setting by one each time, until desired thickness is achieved.

Cutting and Drying Pasta

To cut pasta by hand you need a sharp knife, a fluted-edged pastry wheel, or biscuit or cookie cutter, depending on the type of pasta desired. For strands of pasta, loosely roll up dough like a jelly roll and cut with a knife into desired widths. Rectangular lasagna noodles can be cut out of rolled dough with a knife or, for pretty ripple-edged noodles, use a fluted-edged pastry wheel. Ravioli and tortellini may be cut out of the dough using biscuit cutters. For special occasions, use a heart-shaped cookie cutter to make heart-shaped ravioli for Valentine's Day, a maple leaf or turkey for Thanksgiving, or whatever shape is fitting to the event.

To cut the pasta using a manual pasta machine, pick a desired shape or width. Flour the machine and run thin sheets of pasta through it.

If you plan to cook the pasta that day, hang it on a pasta rack or lay it out on a tea towel or cookie sheet dusted with rice flour for 1 to 5 hours, or until dry. If you want to store the pasta for later use, wrap it around your hand to make a "nest." Put the nest or nests on a cookie sheet or tea towel sprinkled with rice flour, and let the dough dry. Store pasta in an airtight container. It may be refrigerated for a week or frozen for up to a month.

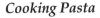

Cooking Pasta

When cooking pasta, use a large pot that has plenty of room for the water to boil and roll. Add pasta to boiling water and stir to prevent sticking. When pasta is *al dente* (firm to the bite, not mushy), remove, drain, and continue with recipe. Since I do not add oil to the pot of boiling water or to the pasta after it cooks, make the sauce first and *then* cook the pasta, adding the sauce immediately after the pasta is drained. This keeps the pasta from sticking to itself. If making pasta salad, cook pasta al dente, drain, submerge in cold water, and drain again.

Homemade, fresh pasta cooks much faster than dried store-bought pasta, so watch and test the pasta while it is cooking to make sure it is not under- or over-done. If using dried store-bought pasta, follow the directions on the package.

Making Stuffed Pasta

Throughout the book, you will be referred back to these pages for instructions on filling, folding, and cutting these common stuffed pastas.

Ravioli

Roll out pasta about $1/8$ inch thick and cut into 4-inch strips. Spoon filling into a pastry bag with a large circle tip. Working with one strip at a time, squeeze out $1/2$ to 1 teaspoon of filling onto the strips of dough at 2-inch intervals. If you do not have a pastry bag, use a teaspoon to place the filling on the dough. Lay another strip of pasta that has been brushed with an egg white mixture (1 egg white mixed with 2 tablespoons water) over the strip of pasta with the filling. Using your fingers or sides of your hands, press pasta together around the mounds of filling.

You can cut the ravioli in squares with a knife or use a pastry wheel, biscuit cutter, or a round ravioli stamp. Put ravioli on a tea towel or cookie sheet sprinkled with rice flour until ready to cook.

Tortellini

Roll out pasta 1/8 inch thick and cut into large rectangles. Cut 3-inch squares or circles from the pasta dough, using a knife or biscuit cutter. Put a level teaspoon of filling in the center of each piece of dough. Moisten edges of dough with water or egg white mixture (1 egg white mixed with 2 tablespoons water). If you cut squares, fold each square over into a triangle, and pinch edges together. Moisten the two corners of the fold, and fold around your forefinger, and pinch together. Continue until all are done. After awhile, you can develop a rhythm and get quite good at this. If you cut circles (using a 3-inch biscuit cutter), place filling on center of circle. Moisten edges of circle and fold over to make a half-circle. Press the edges together. Moisten the two corners and fold them around your forefinger. Pinch together.

Cannelloni or Manicotti

Roll out pasta 1/8 inch thick and cut into 4-inch wide strips. Cut each strip at 3-inch intervals. Put a couple tablespoons of filling on the long side of dough. Gently roll up like a jelly roll. Put into a prepared pan, seam side down. If using commercial cannelloni or manicotti tubes, fill using a pastry bag with a large circle tip.

Using Wonton or Egg Roll Wrappers

Wonton or egg roll wrappers are a fast and satisfactory substitute for fresh, homemade pasta. To use in making ravioli, put a couple teaspoons of filling on one wrapper, moisten another with egg white mixture (1 egg white mixed with 2 tablespoons water), and press edges together. For cannelloni or manicotti, fill and roll according to the instructions above. The wrappers can also be used to make tortellini or in place of lasagna noodles.

Pasta Varieties

Pasta comes in many different shapes. Among those used in this book are the following:

Cannelloni:	large tubes of pasta that can be stuffed with filling.
Capellini:	also known as angel hair, the thinnest of all pastas.
Cavatappi:	a pasta variety shaped like corkscrews, similar to but smaller than fusilli.
Conchiglie:	rounded "seashells" that come in many sizes, from very small to large. The larger shells can be stuffed with filling.
Farfalle:	a small pasta, shaped like a bow.
Fettuccine:	flat, narrow ribbons of pasta cut in $1/5$ -inch widths.
Fusilli:	spiral-shaped pasta that resemble corkscrews.
Gemellini:	two short pieces of pasta twisted together.
Gnocchi:	dumplings traditionally made with potato.
Lasagna:	broad strips of pasta with smooth or rippled edges.
Linguine:	a thin flat pasta, $1/8$ inch wide.
Macaroni:	little tubes of pasta. Elbow macaroni is a slightly curved tube pasta that resembles a bent elbow.

Manicotti:	tubes of pasta that can be stuffed with filling.
Orzo:	rice-shaped pasta used in soups, timbales, and pilafs.
Pappardelle:	flat, broad noodles with fluted edges that are cut in 3/4 -inch widths.
Penne:	small tubes of pasta with pointed ends resembling quill pen tips.
Radiatori:	pasta variety that resembles wall radiators.
Ravioli:	stuffed pasta that can be shaped in squares or circles.
Rigatoni:	large, ridged tube pasta.
Ruote:	small pasta that resembles wagon wheels.
Spaghetti:	long, thin pasta strands that come in different sizes, from very thin to thick.
Tagliatelle:	very thin, flat noodles about 1/4 inch wide.
Tagliolini:	a thin, flat pasta cut in 1/12-inch widths.
Tortellini:	little stuffed pastas that are ring-shaped.
Ziti:	small, thin tubes of pasta.

Basic Ingredients

Here are some basic ingredients I call for in the recipes that follow.

Broths   Homemade broths (that have been defatted) provide the best flavor. Canned broths are an acceptable substitute, but remember to defat before using. If you do not have homemade fish broth handy, you can substitute canned clam juice.

Canadian Bacon   This very lean meat is low in fat. Just a little gives a nice smoky flavor to those dishes that commonly call for bacon or ham.

Cheeses   I call for shredded nonfat cheeses in many recipes. I suggest you test these cheeses and find the ones that work best. For example, some brands or types melt and some don't, some have a nice texture and others are rubbery. Take the time to experiment and find a couple reliable ones.

Chicken or Beef Soup Base   This is a powdered product sold in the spice section of markets. A teaspoon added to a sauce adds lots of flavor with little fat. It is more concentrated than bouillon.

Dried Cheeses   You can get a lot of flavor with little fat by using dried cheeses. Use different types for variety. Some popular kinds are Parmesan, Romano, Asiago, pecorino, dry Jack, Kasseri, or dried ricotta cheese (Mitzithra).

Dried Tomato Flakes   Available as Tomato Splash, these flakes add richness to broths and sauces.

Flour   All-purpose unbleached flour, semolina flour, and whole wheat flour are used. Rice flour is called for when drying pasta. It does not stick to the pasta so that when cooked, the noodles do not become gummy.

Fresh Herbs   Fresh herbs add great flavor to dishes. Dried herbs work wonderfully when dishes or sauces are cooked for long periods of time. But for ultimate flavor, use fresh herbs and spices.

Liquid Smoke Flavoring   This ingredient adds a smoky flavor to dishes without fat.

Nonfat and Lowfat Products   Cottage cheese, sour cream, yogurt, milk, and evaporated milk are all available in both lowfat and nonfat forms. They do require care when cooking to make great sauces and fillings. When baking a dish, I stick to lowfat dairy products because the nonfat products may separate when cooked. Nonfat products should be added at the end of a recipe and warmed over very low heat, never reaching a boil, or sauce will separate.

Oils   Cutting fat and not flavor means using small amounts of strong-flavored oils, such as virgin olive oil, sesame oil, walnut oil, hazelnut oil, and avocado oil.

Roasted Garlic   Put 1 head of garlic in an ovenproof dish (like a custard cup), and add 3 tablespoons broth, cover tightly with foil, and cook in a 300 degree oven for 1 1/2 hours.

Strained Nonfat Yogurt   This is a process celebrity chef Graham Kerr has been noted for, but that many of us have used for years with both yogurt and heavy cream. Put plain nonfat yogurt into a strainer lined with cheesecloth or into a coffee filter. Set the strainer over a bowl and place in the refrigerator overnight. In the morning, discard the liquid accumulated in the bottom of the bowl and reserve the solid yogurt left in the cheesecloth or filter. This wonderful ingredient adds creaminess without fat.

Tomatoes   For a good sauce, tomatoes need to be ripe and flavorful—not pink and mushy. I can 100 quarts of tomatoes each summer so that I have sweet, vine-ripened tomatoes all year. If you don't can your own, use canned whole tomatoes or fresh Italian plum tomatoes, which are pretty good year-round.

1

Basic
Homemade
Pasta

W hen I make homemade pasta, I make quite a bit. In
the following recipes, I use 3 cups of flour as my
starting point. If you are making lasagna, ravioli, tortellini, or
cannelloni, you may have pasta dough left over. Just cut the
extra dough into fettucini or angel hair and dry or freeze for
future use.

Basic Egg Pasta

This recipe is also the framework for the variety of flavored pastas that follow.

Makes 8 to 10 servings
(about 1 1/2 pounds)

3 cups all-purpose unbleached flour
5 large eggs
1 teaspoon salt
1 tablespoon of water or olive oil

Follow the instructions listed under "Making Pasta Dough" in the Introduction (page 2). Roll and cut as desired.

❖

	Each serving provides:		
174	Calories	29 g	Carbohydrate
7 g	Protein	107 mg	Cholesterol
3 g	Fat	1 g	Dietary Fiber

Flavored Pastas

To the Basic Egg Pasta recipe, add what is listed below, taking careful note of changes to the number of eggs used or amount of water or oil included.

Artichoke Pasta: Use 3 eggs. Add one 6-ounce jar of artichoke bottoms, drained and puréed.

Basil and Garlic Pasta: Add 3 tablespoons minced basil and 6 large garlic cloves, chopped fine.

Beet Pasta: Use 2 eggs. Add 1 cup drained canned beets, puréed.

Black Pepper Pasta: Add 4 tablespoons cracked black pepper.

Cornmeal Pasta: Substitute 1 cup cornmeal for 1 cup of the all-purpose unbleached flour.

Curry Pasta: Omit water or oil. Add 1 to 4 tablespoons curry paste, to taste. I like using curry paste for its robust flavor and because of how nicely it blends with the other ingredients.

Dried Tomato Pasta: Omit water or oil. Used dried tomatoes that are *not* bottled in olive oil. Reconstitute 1/3 cup dried tomatoes in 1/2 cup very hot water. Squeeze dry and purée with eggs. Add to rest of ingredients.

Fire-Roasted Red Pepper Pasta: Use 2 eggs. Add 6 ounces (1 jar) roasted red peppers, drained and puréed.

Hot Paprika Pasta: Add 2 to 4 teaspoons hot paprika, to taste.

Jalapeño Pasta: Use 2 eggs. Add one 4-ounce can of diced jalapeños, drained and puréed.

Lemon Pasta: Use 4 eggs. Add 6 tablespoons lemon juice and 3 tablespoons lemon zest.

Mushroom Pasta: Use 3 eggs. Cook 1 cup sliced washed mushrooms in a pan until water in mushrooms evaporates. Purée mushrooms, and blend with eggs. Add to remaining ingredients.

Orange Pasta: Use 4 eggs. Add 6 tablespoons frozen orange juice concentrate and 3 tablespoons orange zest.

Roasted Garlic Pasta: Use 3 eggs. Roast 2 whole garlic heads (see "Basic Ingredients" in Introduction, page 10). Squeeze garlic from cloves, and blend with eggs. Add to rest of ingredients.

Saffron Pasta: Add 1 teaspoon saffron.

Semolina Pasta: Substitute 1 cup semolina flour for 1 cup of the all-purpose unbleached flour.

Spinach Pasta: Use 3 eggs. Cook one 10-ounce package of frozen spinach, drain, and squeeze dry. Purée spinach with eggs. Add mixture to remaining ingredients.

Sweet Potato Pasta: Use 2 eggs. Add 1/2 cup cooked and pureéd sweet potato (or one 6-ounce jar of sweet potato baby food).

Tomato Pasta: Use 2 eggs. Add 1/4 cup tomato paste.

Whole Wheat Pasta: Use half all-purpose unbleached flour and half whole wheat flour.

Egg White Pasta

These egg white noodles fit perfectly into a low-cholesterol diet. To flavor this pasta, follow the directions for flavoring Basic Egg Pasta.

Makes 8 to 10 servings
(about 1 1/2 pounds)

3 cups all-purpose unbleached flour
1 teaspoon salt
5 to 6 large egg whites
1/4 cup water

Follow the instructions listed under "Making Pasta Dough" in the Introduction (page 2). Roll and cut as desired.

Each serving provides:

147	Calories	29 g	Carbohydrate
6 g	Protein	0 mg	Cholesterol
0 g	Fat	1 g	Dietary Fiber

Eggless Pasta

This no-cholesterol pasta cooks very quickly, so watch it carefully.

Makes 8 to 10 servings
(about 1 1/2 pounds)

3 cups all-purpose unbleached flour
1 cup water
1 teaspoon salt

Follow the instructions listed under "Making Pasta Dough" in the Introduction (page 2). Roll and cut as desired.

Each serving provides:

137	Calories	29 g	Carbohydrate
4 g	Protein	0 mg	Cholesterol
0 g	Fat	1 g	Dietary Fiber

Pasta Made with Egg Substitute

This pasta is also good for those watching their cholesterol intake.

Makes 8 to 10 servings
(about 1¹/₂ pounds)

3 cups all-purpose unbleached flour
1 10-ounce carton egg substitute
1 teaspoon salt

Follow the instructions listed under "Making Pasta Dough" in the Introduction (page 2). Roll and cut as desired.

Each serving provides:

149	Calories	29 g	Carbohydrate
6 g	Protein	0 mg	Cholesterol
0 g	Fat	1 g	Dietary Fiber

Chocolate Pasta

Chocolate pasta can be cut in angel hair and served drizzled with a nonfat chocolate or caramel sauce. It can also be cut into noodles to use in a ricotta dessert lasagna or a kugel. By using cocoa instead of chocolate, the fat content is lowered without the loss of rich chocolate flavor.

Makes 8 servings

2 cups all-purpose unbleached flour
$3/4$ cup cocoa
$3/4$ cup confectioners' sugar
pinch of salt
$3/4$ cup egg substitute

Follow the instructions listed under "Making Pasta Dough" in the Introduction. If using a food processor, do not let the machine knead the dough. Remove dough from work bowl and knead by hand on a floured work surface until smooth and not sticky. Shape dough into a ball and wrap in plastic wrap. Let rest for 20 minutes. Roll and cut as desired.

❖

Each serving provides:

180	Calories	38 g	Carbohydrate
7 g	Protein	0 mg	Cholesterol
2 g	Fat	1 g	Dietary Fiber

Spicy Pumpkin Pasta

I use this pasta in Spicy Pumpkin Pasta in Whiskey Yogurt Sauce (p. 276). For a savory version, omit the sugar and pumpkin pie spice and serve with a wild mushroom sauce spiked with rum or whiskey.

Makes 8–10 servings
(about 1 1/2 pounds)

3 cups all-purpose unbleached flour
1/4 cup confectioners' sugar
3 teaspoons pumpkin pie spice
1/2 teaspoon salt
1/2 cup pureéd pumpkin
3 large egg whites

In food processor, process flour, sugar, spice, and salt, or mix by hand in a large bowl. Add pumpkin and egg whites to flour mixture, and blend well. On a floured work surface, knead dough by hand until smooth and not sticky. Add a little water if dough is dry. Shape dough into a ball and wrap in plastic wrap. Let rest for 20 minutes. Roll and cut as desired.

❖

Each serving provides:			
157	Calories	33 g	Carbohydrate
5 g	Protein	0 mg	Cholesterol
0 g	Fat	1 g	Dietary Fiber

2

Basic Pasta Sauces Made Light

Bolognese Sauce

This sauce was a favorite of mine as a child. My mouth would water as the sauce would bubble on the stove and my mother would let me grate the hard cheese — all in anticipation of the evening meal.

Makes about 6 cups

1 pound lean ground round
1 teaspoon virgin olive oil
1 medium onion, minced
1 carrot, minced
2 stalks celery, minced
1/2 cup defatted beef broth
1 1/2 ounces dried Italian mushrooms, soaked in 1 cup hot water
10 Italian plum tomatoes, peeled and coarsely chopped
1 can (15 ounces) tomato sauce
2 cups water
1 teaspoon sugar
8 large fresh basil leaves, chopped
2 tablespoons chopped fresh oregano
1 teaspoon dried rosemary
1 teaspoon dried thyme
salt and pepper to taste

Sauté meat in oil until all pink is gone. Drain meat, remove from pan and set aside. To the same pan, add onion, carrot, celery, and broth. Cook, uncovered, over medium heat until liquid evaporates. Return meat to pan.

Squeeze mushrooms, reserving liquid they soaked in,
and chop in a food processor or by hand. Add mushrooms,
reserved liquid, and all other ingredients and cook for 30 minutes. This sauce freezes well.

Each 1/2-cup serving provides:

134	Calories	10 g	Carbohydrate
11g	Protein	31 mg	Cholesterol
6 g	Fat	2 g	Dietary Fiber

Light Tomato-Basil Sauce

This is a simple, yet fresh-tasting, sauce. Use oregano, cilantro, marjoram, tarragon, or thyme in place of the basil for a different flavor.

Makes 3 cups

1/3 cup chopped onion
2 cloves garlic, minced
3/4 cup defatted beef broth
8 Italian plum tomatoes, peeled and puréed
1 teaspoon sugar
3 tablespoons minced fresh basil
1/2 cup dry white wine
salt and pepper to taste

Sauté onion and garlic in 1/4 cup of the broth until liquid is evaporated. Add tomatoes, sugar, basil, the remaining 1/2 cup broth, and the wine. Cook, uncovered, over low heat for 10 minutes. Season with salt and pepper to taste and cook 5 minutes more.

Each 1/2-cup serving provides:

30	Calories	5 g	Carbohydrate
1 g	Protein	0 mg	Cholesterol
0 g	Fat	1 g	Dietary Fiber

Pesto Sauce

Try this pesto sauce on pizza or as a spread on your favorite sandwich. Add a little lite evaporated milk and nonfat sour cream to make a delicious pasta sauce. Vary the ingredients to make a range of interesting pestos: substitute spinach for the parsley; mint, sorrel, cilantro, or oregano for the basil; cashews, peanuts, or pine nuts for the almonds; or Asiago, dry Jack, or Romano for the Parmesan.

Makes 1 cup

4 large cloves garlic, peeled
1 cup chopped fresh parsley
1 cup chopped fresh basil
3 tablespoons chopped blanched almonds
2 1/2 tablespoons freshly grated Parmesan cheese
2 1/2 teaspoons virgin olive oil

Put garlic into food processor and pulse until garlic is well chopped. Add parsley, basil, and almonds and pulse until all chopped. Add cheese and olive oil, and blend well.

❖

Each 1/4-cup serving provides:

92	Calories	4 g	Carbohydrate
4 g	Protein	3 mg	Cholesterol
8 g	Fat	2 g	Dietary Fiber

Mushroom Sauce

This scrumptious sauce can top many dishes — let your imagination go wild!

Makes about 2 cups

1 teaspoon butter
1 1/2 cups sliced mushrooms
2 green onions, diced
1/4 cup grated carrot
1/2 teaspoon herbes de Provence
1/2 teaspoon dried thyme leaves
1/4 teaspoon white pepper
1/2 cup defatted beef broth
2/3 cup lite evaporated milk
1/4 cup dry white wine
salt and black pepper to taste
3 teaspoons cornstarch mixed with 2 tablespoons water

In a nonstick pan, cook butter, mushrooms, green onions, carrot, herbs, white pepper, and broth until liquid reduces to about 3 tablespoons. Remove from heat and add evaporated milk, wine, and salt and black pepper to taste. Return to heat and cook over very low heat until sauce is heated through. Stir in cornstarch mixture and blend until sauce thickens.

Each 1/2-cup serving provides:

68	Calories	10 g	Carbohydrate
4 g	Protein	4 mg	Cholesterol
1 g	Fat	1 g	Dietary Fiber

WHITE CREAM SAUCE No. 1

Vary this basic sauce by using different cheeses, spices, or liquors. Or add puréed vegetables and nonfat sour cream.

Makes 2 1/2 cups

3 tablespoons minced onion
1/2 cup defatted chicken broth
2 cups nonfat milk
1/3 cup all-purpose unbleached flour
1/2 cup dry white wine
1 teaspoon chicken soup base
salt and white pepper to taste
3 tablespoons freshly grated Parmesan cheese (optional)

Cook onion and broth in a saucepan and until liquid evaporates.

In a small bowl, whisk flour with milk. Add to pan with onions and whisk, cooking until sauce begins to thicken. Add wine, soup base, and season with salt and pepper. Blend in Parmesan cheese, if using, and cook over low heat for 2 to 3 minutes, until well blended.

Each 1/2-cup serving provides:

84	Calories	12 g	Carbohydrate
5 g	Protein	2 mg	Cholesterol
0 g	Fat	0 g	Dietary Fiber

WHITE CREAM SAUCE NO. 2

This white sauce also has very little fat. You can add other ingredients as I described with White Cream Sauce No. 1.

Makes almost 3 cups

3 tablespoons minced onion
1 cup defatted chicken broth
1 1/2 cups nonfat cottage cheese, puréed until smooth
1/4 cup dry white wine
1/4 cup nonfat sour cream
1 teaspoon chicken soup base
salt and pepper to taste
3 tablespoons freshly grated Parmesan or other hard cheese

Cook onion and 1/2 cup of the broth until liquid evaporates. Stir in the remaining 1/2 cup broth, the cottage cheese, wine, sour cream, and soup base. Cook over very low heat until just blended. Season with salt and pepper to taste. Stir in cheese, blending well.

❖

Each serving provides:

63	Calories	4 g	Carbohydrate
9 g	Protein	5 mg	Cholesterol
1 g	Fat	0 g	Dietary Fiber

3

Pasta Soups

Artichoke Pasta
and Vegetable Soup

*In the spring and summer months, I can not get enough of fresh
artichokes. Artichoke pasta is now available ready-made in many
houseware and gourmet grocery shops.*

Makes 6 servings

$1/2$ cup artichoke pasta, cut into $1/12$-inch-wide tagliolini
     and then cut into 1-inch-long pieces (page 15)
2 leeks, white part only, sliced
6 cups defatted chicken broth
$1/2$ cup thinly sliced celery
1 cup broccoli flowerets, cut small
1 small carrot, cut julienne
$1/2$ cup drained canned lima beans, rinsed
1 teaspoon dried marjoram
1 teaspoon dried savory
1 cup fresh or frozen peas
1 small zucchini, cut julienne
salt and pepper to taste
freshly grated Parmesan cheese for garnish

Cook leeks in $1/4$ cup of the broth until liquid evaporates.
Add the remaining $5\,3/4$ cups broth, celery, broccoli, carrot,
lima beans, marjoram, and savory. Cook, uncovered, over
medium heat for 15 minutes. Add peas and zucchini and cook

5 minutes more. Add pasta and cook until pasta is al dente, about 3 to 5 minutes more. Season with salt and pepper. Ladle soup into serving bowls. Sprinkle a little Parmesan on top of each bowl before serving.

Each serving provides:

116	Calories	21 g	Carbohydrate
7 g	Protein	13 mg	Cholesterol
1 g	Fat	4 g	Dietary Fiber

Calypso Bean and Pasta Soup

Calypso beans — one of my favorites — are black and white, resembling a cow pattern. You can find them in gourmet grocery and houseware shops. Calypsos cook much quicker than other beans, so check for doneness after 25 minutes of cooking. If you are unable to find them, substitute your favorite bean.

Makes 8 servings

1 pound Calypso beans
1 large yellow onion, chopped
3 cloves garlic, minced
8 ounces Canadian bacon, diced
1 sweet red pepper, diced
2 teaspoons butter
$1/8$ teaspoon cayenne pepper
1 teaspoon dried tomato flakes (such as Tomato Splash)
2 tablespoons tomato paste
$1 1/2$ teaspoons dried oregano
6 cups defatted beef broth
$1/2$ cup elbow macaroni

Pick over beans, rinse, and soak in water overnight. Drain when ready to use.

In a large pot, sauté onion, garlic, bacon, and red pepper in butter until onion begins to soften. Add cayenne, dried tomato flakes, tomato paste, oregano, broth, and beans. Cook, uncovered, over medium heat for 25 minutes. Check to see if beans are done. They should be tender but not mushy. Add macaroni and cook for 10 minutes more. Season to taste with salt and pepper.

Each serving provides:

302	Calories	45 g	Carbohydrate
22 g	Protein	19 mg	Cholesterol
4 g	Fat	8 g	Dietary Fiber

Cauliflower and Fennel Soup with Pasta

Adding roasted onion to this dish makes the broth very rich and delicious. Try adding puréed roasted onion to your mashed potatoes next Thanksgiving. You'll love it.

Makes 8 servings

1 large onion
4 cups defatted chicken broth
2 cups nonfat milk
1 teaspoon dried chervil
$1/2$ cup small tube pasta, such as elbow macaroni
2 cups chopped cauliflower
1 cup chopped fennel bulb
white pepper and salt to taste

Preheat oven to 350 degrees.

Leave skin on onion and put into a baking dish. Pour $1/2$ cup of the broth over the onion and cook for 60 minutes. When onion is cool enough to handle, remove skin, cut off ends of onion, and purée.

Whisk together the remaining $3 1/2$ cups of the broth and milk with the onion purée and blend well. Add the chervil and pasta and cook over low heat until pasta is done, about 8 minutes. Set aside.

In a pot of boiling water, cook cauliflower and fennel about 15 minutes, or until tender. Drain and purée in a blender or food processor. Stir purée into soup and mix well. Season with salt and pepper to taste. Cook for 3 minutes to develop flavors.

❖

	Each serving provides:		
73	Calories	13 g	Carbohydrate
5 g	Protein	1 mg	Cholesterol
0 g	Fat	1 g	Dietary Fiber

Navy Bean, Chard, and Pasta Soup

This is a nice, hearty soup. Canadian bacon is very lean and a good substitute for high-fat bacon.

Makes 10 servings

3 leeks, white part only, sliced
6 cups defatted chicken broth
2 carrots, diced
1 16-ounce can whole tomatoes, diced
6 ounces diced Canadian bacon
1 can (15 ounces) navy beans, rinsed and drained
$^1/_8$ teaspoon fennel seeds, crushed
$^1/_2$ teaspoon dried thyme leaves
$^1/_2$ cup dry sherry
4 cups Swiss chard, cut into $^1/_2$-inch pieces
$^1/_2$ cup gnocchi-shaped pasta

Put leeks and $1/2$ cup of the broth in a soup pot and cook
until liquid evaporates. Add remaining $5^1/2$ cups of the broth,
carrots, tomatoes, bacon, beans, fennel seeds, and thyme. Cook,
covered, over low heat for 30 minutes. Add sherry, chard, and
pasta and cook for 15 minutes, or until pasta is al dente.

❖

Each serving provides:

139	Calories	19 g	Carbohydrate
9 g	Protein	10 mg	Cholesterol
2 g	Fat	3 g	Dietary Fiber

Saffron Tortellini Soup

Supermarkets that carry fresh pasta usually offer a lowfat ricotta tortellini or ravioli.

Makes 6 servings

2 onions, diced small
2 teaspoons sugar
8 cups defatted beef broth
2 tablespoons balsamic vinegar
1 carrot, minced
1 celery stalk, minced
1/4 cup chopped fresh parsley
1/4 to 1/2 teaspoon saffron to taste
9 ounces ricotta tortellini
salt and pepper to taste

Cook onions, sugar, 1/2 cup of the broth, and vinegar in a non-stick pan on very low heat until liquid evaporates and onions begin to brown slightly. Add the remaining 7 1/2 cups broth, carrot, celery, and parsley. Cook, uncovered, over medium heat for 2 to 3 minutes, or until vegetables are fork-tender. Stir in saffron and add tortellini, and salt and pepper to taste. Cook until tortellini are done according to package directions.

Each serving provides:

178	Calories	27 g	Carbohydrate
10 g	Protein	49 mg	Cholesterol
4 g	Fat	3 g	Dietary Fiber

Stuffed Ravioli in Light Beef Broth

This is a great meal to serve when you have very little time to cook.

Makes 4 servings

1 small onion, minced
1 small carrot, shredded
1 stalk celery, minced
2 tablespoons minced fresh parsley
1 1/2 tablespoons dried tomato flakes (such as Tomato Splash)
2 3/4 cups defatted beef broth
1/2 cup slivered Swiss chard
salt and pepper to taste
1 package (9 ounces) lowfat ravioli
2 tablespoons freshly grated Romano cheese for garnish

Cook onion, carrot, celery, parsley, and dried tomato flakes in
3/4 cup of the broth over medium heat until liquid evaporates.
Add the remaining 2 cups broth and the chard and cook for 10
minutes more. Season with salt and pepper to taste.

Meanwhile, cook ravioli according to package instructions. Drain and put a portion of the ravioli into each soup bowl and pour beef broth over ravioli. Garnish with the Romano.

Each serving provides:

217	Calories	31 g	Carbohydrate
13 g	Protein	46 mg	Cholesterol
4 g	Fat	3 g	Dietary Fiber

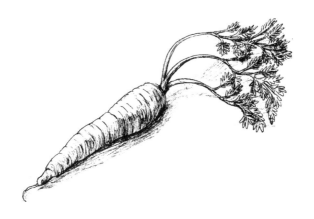

Spinach and Tomato Soup with Angel Hair

This soup is deliciously light and quick to prepare.

Makes 6 servings

1/2 onion, chopped
2 cloves garlic, chopped
2 tablespoons chopped fresh basil
2 large ripe tomatoes, peeled, seeded, and chopped fine
4 1/4 cups vegetable broth
2 cups slivered spinach with stems removed
6 ounces angel hair pasta, broken into 2-inch pieces
salt and pepper to taste

Over low heat, sauté onion and garlic in 1/4 cup of the broth until liquid is almost all evaporated. Add basil, tomato, and the remaining 4 cups broth and simmer for 10 minutes. Add spinach and pasta and cook for 3 to 4 minutes, or until pasta is done. Season with salt and pepper to taste.

Each serving provides:

144	Calories	30 g	Carbohydrate
5 g	Protein	0 mg	Cholesterol
1 g	Fat	2 g	Dietary Fiber

4

Pasta Salads

Fusilli with Chunky Gazpacho Dressing

This is a delicious and refreshing salad to serve when vegetables are fresh and bountiful. If you don't have ripe tomatoes available, use fresh Italian plum tomatoes. I like to serve this salad with toasted baguettes spread with roasted garlic.

Makes 12 servings

1 pound fusilli or other corkscrew pasta
4 medium fresh tomatoes, peeled, seeded, and diced small
1 cucumber, cut in half, seeds removed, and diced small
4 green onions, sliced
1 medium sweet yellow pepper, diced small
1 jalapeño pepper, minced
1 large stalk celery, diced small
2 tablespoons chopped fresh basil
1 tablespoon chopped fresh chervil
1/3 cup tomato juice
1/4 cup balsamic vinegar
juice of 1 lemon
1 tablespoon virgin olive oil
1 teaspoon Worcestershire sauce
1/2 teaspoon sugar
salt and coarsely ground pepper to taste

Cook fusilli until al dente. Rinse under cold water, drain, and set in a large bowl. Add tomatoes, cucumbers, green onions, yellow pepper, jalapeño, celery, basil, and chervil to pasta and mix well.

Whisk together tomato juice, vinegar, lemon juice, olive oil, Worcestershire sauce, sugar, and salt and pepper to taste. Pour dressing over pasta and vegetables and toss.

Each serving provides:

167	Calories	33 g	Carbohydrate
5 g	Protein	0 mg	Cholesterol
2 g	Fat	4 g	Dietary Fiber

Grilled Chicken and Pasta Salad with Ginger Dressing

This is one of my favorite salads for summer. I like to serve it in a pineapple boat.

Makes 6 main-dish servings or 10 side-dish servings

3 teaspoons garlic paste
2 teaspoons lemon juice
1 teaspoon sesame oil
4 chicken breasts, boned and skinned
10 ounces fusilli or other corkscrew pasta
1 cup diced fresh pineapple
3/4 cup green grapes, cut in half
1 small sweet red pepper, chopped
1/2 cup fresh bean sprouts, blanched
1/4 cup sliced green onion
3 tablespoons dry roasted peanuts
1/2 cup rice vinegar
1/3 cup frozen pineapple juice concentrate
1 tablespoon honey
1 teaspoon grated fresh ginger
1/4 teaspoon chili paste
1 head red leaf lettuce, slivered

Mix garlic paste, lemon juice, and sesame oil together. Rub on chicken. Marinate for 15 minutes. Grill chicken about 6 minutes a side, or until desired doneness. Slice chicken in 1/2-inch slices and then cut slices in half. Set aside.

Cook fusilli according to package directions. Rinse under cold water, drain, and set in a large bowl. Add pineapple, grapes, red pepper, sprouts, green onion, and peanuts to fusilli and toss.

Whisk together vinegar, concentrate, honey, ginger, and chili paste until well blended. Pour dressing over pasta and vegetables and toss well. Carefully add chicken and toss a couple times. Serve on a bed of the slivered lettuce.

Each main-dish serving provides:

224	Calories	32 g	Carbohydrate
16 g	Protein	29 mg	Cholesterol
4 g	Fat	3 g	Dietary Fiber

Niçoise Salad with Rigatoni

A delicious pasta salad with flavors from the south of France. Soaking the anchovy fillets in milk removes some of their saltiness.

Makes 6 servings

2 anchovy fillets (optional)
1/4 cup milk (optional)
8 ounces rigatoni
3 teaspoons virgin olive oil
1 can (6 ounces) water-packed white tuna, drained
1/3 cup Niçoise olives, drained
1/2 small red onion, cut into rings
1 tablespoon drained tiny capers
1 cup green beans, cut on the diagonal
1/3 cup balsamic vinegar
2 tablespoons lemon juice
1 teaspoon sugar
1 teaspoon celery seed
1 teaspoon dry mustard
1 tablespoon *each* chopped fresh tarragon, basil, and parsley
1/4 cup nonfat sour cream
salt and pepper to taste
1 head romaine lettuce, torn into bite-size pieces
2 medium tomatoes, each cut into 8 wedges

If using anchovy fillets, soak in milk for 15 minutes. Drain and chop. Set aside.

Cook rigatoni according to package directions. Rinse in cold water, drain, and set into a large bowl. Toss with 1 teaspoon of

the olive oil. Add tuna, olives, red onion, capers, and green
beans and toss gently.

In a blender, mix optional anchovies, the remaining 2 teaspoons of the olive oil, vinegar, lemon juice, sugar, celery seed,
mustard, herbs, sour cream, and salt and pepper to taste. Pour
dressing over rigatoni mixture and toss.

Put lettuce on a platter and mound with pasta salad.
Arrange tomatoes in a pinwheel pattern on top of the salad.

❖

Each serving provides:

264	Calories	39 g	Carbohydrate
15 g	Protein	8 mg	Cholesterol
6 g	Fat	5 g	Dietary Fiber

Pasta, Potato, and Fennel Salad with Smoky Mustard Dressing

Bring this unusual dish the next time you're asked to bring potato salad to a picnic. Your hosts will be pleasantly surprised.

Makes 8 servings

8 ounces fusilli or other corkscrew pasta
1 pound little new potatoes, cooked and quartered
1 large fennel bulb, diced
2 tablespoons chopped fresh parsley
1 tablespoon chopped fresh mint
1 cup peas, cooked and drained
2 medium carrots, diced and blanched
4 ounces smoked turkey, diced
3 tablespoons nonfat sour cream
1 tablespooon reduced-fat mayonnaise
1 to 3 teaspoons Dijon mustard or to taste
$1/2$ teaspoon lemon pepper
salt to taste
$1/4$ cup rice vinegar
1 teaspoon Worchestershire sauce
2 to 3 drops liquid smoke flavoring
1 teaspoon sugar
1 head green leaf lettuce

Prepare pasta according to package directions. Rinse under cold water, drain, and place in a large bowl. Add the potatoes,

fennel, parsley, mint, peas, carrots, and turkey to the pasta
and toss.

Blend other ingredients except lettuce in a blender or food
processor and mix with pasta. When ready to serve, line a plate
with the lettuce and mound with the pasta salad.

Each serving provides:

216	Calories	40 g	Carbohydrate
9 g	Protein	7 mg	Cholesterol
2 g	Fat	6 g	Dietary Fiber

Grilled Eggplant Salad with Asian Noodles

I put my favorite oils into spray bottles; I end up using much less oil.

Makes 4 servings

2 Japanese eggplants
1/2 pound asparagus
1/2 cup julienned jicama
3 green onions, sliced thinly on the diagonal
1/2 cup (2 ounces) snap peas, blanched
1 small carrot, cut julienne
2 tablespoons chopped fresh cilantro
4 ounces thin Asian noodles
2 tablespoons minced onion
1/2 cup rice vinegar
1 teaspoon sesame oil
2 teaspoons soy sauce
1/2 teaspoon grated fresh ginger
1 tablespoon sugar

Cut eggplants in half lengthwise and spray lightly with olive oil spray. Clean asparagus and bend stalks to snap where tender part begins. Discard the tough bottom half. Spray asparagus with olive oil spray. Grill eggplant and asparagus over very hot coals so that grill lines will appear quickly, about 2–3 minutes. Do not overcook. Remove and let cool slightly. Dice eggplant and cut asparagus in 1-inch slices. Place in a large bowl. Add jicama, onions, snap peas, carrot, and cilantro and toss.

Cook noodles according to package directions. Rinse under cold water and drain. Toss noodles with vegetables.

In a blender or food processor, blend onion, rice vinegar, sesame oil, soy sauce, ginger, and sugar. Pour dressing over salad and toss.

Each serving provides:

167	Calories	32 g	Carbohydrate
6 g	Protein	0 mg	Cholesterol
2 g	Fat	3 g	Dietary Fiber

Artichoke Pasta Salad with Scallops

This salad is at its most flavorful when the dressing is slightly warmed.

Makes 4 servings

8 ounces Artichoke Pasta, cut into angel hair (page 15)
2 teaspoons virgin olive oil
12 ounces scallops
2 cloves garlic, chopped
1 teaspoon sesame oil
2 medium tomatoes, peeled, seeded, and diced
3 tablespoons chopped fresh parsley
1 tablespoon chopped fresh basil
2 teaspoons sugar
$1/3$ cup white wine vinegar
1 teaspoon dry mustard
1 teaspoon black sesame seeds (optional)
salt and pepper to taste
1 head Bibb lettuce

Make pasta and cook until al dente. Rinse under cold water, drain, and place in a large bowl. Toss pasta with 1 teaspoon of the olive oil.

    Sauté the scallops and garlic in the other teaspoon of olive oil and the sesame oil for about 1 1/2 minutes. Add the tomato,

❖

parsley, basil, sugar, vinegar, mustard, and optional sesame seeds. Season to taste with salt and pepper.

Arrange lettuce on a platter or on individual plates. Place pasta on the lettuce and pour the scallops with sauce over the pasta. Serve immediately.

❖

Each serving provides:

274	Calories	34 g	Carbohydrate
20 g	Protein	83 mg	Cholesterol
6 g	Fat	2 g	Dietary Fiber

Shrimp and Snap Pea Salad with Oriental Dressing

This tangy and sweet dressing is delightful with shrimp.

Makes 6 servings

12 ounces Jalapeño Pasta, cut into fettuccine (page 16)
2 teaspoons virgin olive oil
1 pound large shrimp, peeled and deveined
3 cloves garlic, minced
1 teaspoon sesame oil
1 medium carrot, sliced thinly on the diagonal
1 1/2 cups (6 ounces) fresh snap peas
1 small sweet red pepper, slivered
1/4 cup defatted chicken broth
2 teaspoons chopped fresh anise (the top part of a fennel bulb)
3 tablespoons seedless raspberry jam
1/2 cup seasoned rice vinegar
1 tablespoon soy sauce
1/3 cup strained nonfat yogurt (see page 10)
salt and pepper to taste

Prepare pasta and cut into 4-inch pieces. Cook until al dente. Rinse under cold water, drain, and place in a large bowl. Toss pasta with 1 teaspoon of the olive oil. Put on a platter or divide among 6 plates.

Using a sharp knife, cut shrimp along the back where the vein was, almost through to the other side. Open up shrimp at the cut to make a plumper-looking shrimp. Sauté shrimp and garlic in a very hot pan with the remaining teaspoon of olive oil and the sesame oil, until shrimp turn pink and are done. Remove shrimp to a bowl.

In same pan, cook carrot, snap peas, red pepper, and broth until liquid evaporates. Mix with shrimp and spoon over pasta.

Whisk together the anise, jam, vinegar, soy sauce, yogurt, and salt and pepper to taste. Drizzle over salad.

Each serving provides:

281	Calories	40 g	Carbohydrate
19 g	Protein	153 mg	Cholesterol
4 g	Fat	3 g	Dietary Fiber

Crab and Pasta Salad with Cucumber-Tarragon Dressing

When cutting fat in recipes, use small amounts of stronger oils, such as virgin olive oil, to give low-fat dishes more flavor.

Makes 10 servings

1 pound medium pasta shells
1 tablespoon virgin olive oil
1 pound crabmeat
$1/2$ cup chopped fresh parsley
1 medium sweet red pepper, slivered
$1/2$ cup sliced green onion
$1/3$ cup pine nuts
1 cucumber, peeled, seeded, and minced
1 tablespoon fresh minced tarragon
1 teaspoon Dijon mustard
1 teaspoon Worcestershire sauce
$1/2$ cup tarragon vinegar
2 tablespoons reduced-fat mayonnaise
$1/4$ cup nonfat sour cream
salt and pepper to taste

Cook pasta according to package directions. Rinse in cold water, drain, and toss with olive oil. Add crabmeat, parsley, red pepper, green onion, and pine nuts.

In a small bowl, mix remaining ingredients. Pour over pasta and mix well. Cover and refrigerate until ready to serve. Toss again before serving.

❖

Each serving provides:

248	Calories	35 g	Carbohydrate
16 g	Protein	48 mg	Cholesterol
5 g	Fat	4 g	Dietary Fiber

Spinach Pasta Salad with Garlicky Caper Dressing

The striking colors of this salad make a beautiful presentation.

Makes 8 servings

8 ounces Spinach Pasta, cut into fettuccine (page 17)
1/4 cup sliced black olives, rinsed and drained
1 sweet red pepper, diced
1 cup cauliflower flowerets, cut small and blanched
16 yellow pear tomatoes
2 small heads radicchio, separate the leaves of one head and
     thinly slice the other
2 cloves garlic, minced
2 teaspoons walnut oil
1/2 cup nonfat cottage cheese
1 teaspoon sugar
3 tablespoons tarragon vinegar
3 tablespoons drained tiny capers, chopped
1 to 3 teaspoons Dijon mustard or to taste
2 tablespoons chopped fresh parsley
salt and pepper to taste

Make pasta and cook until al dente. Rinse under cold water, drain, and place in a large bowl. Add olives, red pepper, cauliflower, tomatoes, and sliced radicchio.

Line a platter or bowl with the radicchio leaves.

Whisk together garlic, oil, cottage cheese, sugar, vinegar, ca-pers, mustard, parsley, and salt and pepper. Pour the dressing over the pasta and vegetables and toss well. Place tossed salad on radicchio leaves.

❖

Each serving provides:

130	Calories	21 g	Carbohydrate
6 g	Protein	28 mg	Cholesterol
3 g	Fat	2 g	Dietary Fiber

Angel Hair and Snapper Salad with Leek-Mango Dressing

I like to use Hot Paprika Pasta (page 16) or Lemon Pasta (page 16) for this recipe. Packaged angel hair pasta is also fine to use.

Makes 10 servings

12 ounces angel hair pasta
1 cup chopped celery
1 sweet yellow pepper, cut julienne
1 cup quartered cherry tomatoes
12 ounces red snapper
1 small leek, white part only, sliced
1 mango, peeled, seeded, and minced
1 clove garlic, minced
1/3 cup defatted chicken broth
1/2 teaspoon coriander seed, crushed
1 teaspoon celery seed
1 tablespoon minced fresh dill
1 teaspoon Dijon mustard
juice of 2 lemons
2 tablespoons white wine vinegar
1 tablespoon reduced-fat mayonnaise
1/4 cup strained nonfat yogurt (page 10)
salt and pepper to taste
1 head Bibb lettuce

Make pasta of choice and cook until al dente. Rinse under cold water, drain, and place in a large bowl. Add celery, yellow pepper, and tomatoes.

Spray a grill and the snapper with olive oil spray. Grill over hot coals until the snapper flakes and is done. Remove snapper from grill and let cool. Cut into thin strips. Set aside.

Cook leek, mango, garlic, and broth over low heat until liquid evaporates. Remove to a blender and purée. Let sit 10 minutes to cool.

In a small bowl, whisk together leek purée, coriander seed, celery seed, dill, mustard, lemon juice, vinegar, mayonnaise, and yogurt until well blended. Season with salt and pepper. Pour dressing over pasta and toss. Carefully fold in snapper. Serve on a platter decorated with the lettuce.

Each serving provides:

194	Calories	32 g	Carbohydrate
12 g	Protein	13 mg	Cholesterol
2g	Fat	3 g	Dietary Fiber

Chunky Chicken and Pasta Salad with Kiwi Dressing

Sesame oil or walnut oil are both good in this recipe. Sesame oil has a little stronger taste, so less can be used.

Makes 12 servings

6 chicken breasts
1/4 cup dry white wine
1 bay leaf
3 peppercorns
1 pound corkscrew pasta
1/4 cup chopped walnuts
2 teaspoons sugar
1 cup diced fresh pineapple
2 medium apples, diced and tossed with 1 tablespoon
    lemon juice
1 cup green or red seedless grapes, cut in half
3 kiwi, peeled and diced
2 tablespoons honey
1 teaspoon sesame oil or 3 teaspoons walnut oil
1/2 cup pineapple juice
1/4 cup nonfat sour cream
1 tablespoon minced fresh mint
salt and pepper to taste

Place chicken in a saucepan. Cover with water, add wine, bay leaf and peppercorns. Cook, covered, over medium-high heat until chicken is done, about 15 minutes. Take chicken out of pan. Remove skin and bones. Dice and refrigerate until cold, about 1 hour.

Meanwhile, prepare pasta according to package directions. Rinse under cold water, drain, and set aside in a large bowl.

Put walnuts and sugar in a nonstick pan. Toast walnuts over low heat, shaking pan to prevent burning or sticking. Add walnuts, chicken, pineapple, apples, and grapes to the pasta and toss. To make dressing, blend kiwi, honey, oil, and juice in a blender. Then blend in sour cream, mint, and salt and pepper to taste. Pour dressing over pasta and fruit and toss.

Each serving provides:

280	Calories	43 g	Carbohydrate
19 g	Protein	37 mg	Cholesterol
4 g	Fat	4 g	Dietary Fiber

Southwestern Bean and Pasta Salad

With your summer garden bounty, make this festive garden salad with a southwestern flavor.

Makes 8 servings

8 small corn tortillas
8 ounces bow-shaped pasta
2 ears fresh corn on the cob or 1 package (9 ounces) frozen
    whole kernel corn, defrosted
$1/2$ pound tender fresh green beans, blanched and sliced in
    1-inch pieces
1 can (15 ounces) black beans, washed and drained
2 medium zucchini, sliced thin and blanched
1 small jicama, cut julienne
12 cherry tomatoes, cut in half
2 teaspoons corn oil
$3/4$ cup good-quality salsa
$1/2$ teaspoon fennel seed
$1/4$ cup nonfat sour cream
2 tablespoons reduced-fat mayonnaise
salt and pepper to taste

Preheat oven to 400 degrees.

    Steam tortillas until they are soft. Put the tortillas into muffin tins that have been sprayed with vegetable spray. Press tortillas into tins, forming little cups. Spray the tops with water and bake for 8 to 10 minutes, or until crisp. Remove cups and let cool before filling with the bean salad.

Meanwhile, prepare pasta according to package directions. Rinse under cold water, drain, and set aside.

If using fresh corn, blanch and cut kernels off cob. Combine corn, green beans, black beans, zucchini, jicama, tomatoes, pasta, and corn oil in a large bowl.

In a blender, mix together salsa, fennel seed, sour cream, and mayonnaise and blend well. Season to taste with salt and pepper. Pour over pasta and toss. Fill tortilla cups with salad and serve.

Each serving provides:

297	Calories	57 g	Carbohydrate
10 g	Protein	3 mg	Cholesterol
4 g	Fat	8 g	Dietary Fiber

Grilled Vegetable
and Red Pepper Pasta Salad

Makes 8 servings

10 ounces Fire-Roasted Red Pepper Pasta, cut into fettuccine
   (page 16)
2 tablespoons virgin olive oil
2 small Japanese eggplants, cut in half lengthwise
1 sweet yellow pepper, cut in half and seeds removed
8 asparagus spears
12 tiny baby carrots, cleaned or 2 large carrots, cut into 3-inch
   julienne
2 small zucchini, sliced in half lengthwise
2 tablespoons balsamic vinegar
1/2 cup strained nonfat yogurt (page 10)
2 cloves garlic, minced
2 tablespoons minced fresh basil
1 teaspoon sugar
1/2 to 1 teaspoon Dijon mustard or to taste
salt and pepper to taste

Make pasta and cook until al dente. Rinse under cold water,
drain, and place in a large bowl. Toss with 1 tablespoon of the
olive oil.

   Rub vegetables with the remaining tablespoon of olive oil.
Grill vegetables over very hot coals until grill marks appear.
Dice vegetables and set aside.

In a blender, mix vinegar, yogurt, garlic, basil, sugar, mustard, and salt and pepper to taste and blend well. Pour dressing over pasta and toss.

Each serving provides:

164	Calories	26 g	Carbohydrate
5 g	Protein	24 mg	Cholesterol
5 g	Fat	2 g	Dietary Fiber

Penne Salad with Tahini Dressing

Tahini is a peanut butter-like spread made with sesame seeds and is found in the health-food sections of most grocery stores.

Makes 10 servings

1 pound penne
2 teaspoons sesame oil
1 large sweet yellow pepper, diced
1 large carrot, shredded
$^1/_2$ cup sliced green onions
$^1/_2$ cup sliced water chestnuts
1 medium head radicchio, slivered
3 tablespoons chopped fresh Chinese basil or regular basil
2 teaspoons tahini
1 tablespoon soy sauce
$^1/_2$ cup rice vinegar
2 tablespoons lemon juice
1 tablespoon honey
salt and pepper to taste

Prepare pasta according to package directions. Rinse under cold water, drain, and place in a large bowl. Toss with the sesame oil. Add yellow pepper, carrot, green onion, chestnuts, radicchio, and basil.

Whisk together the tahini, soy sauce, vinegar, lemon juice, honey, and salt and pepper. Pour dressing over pasta and toss.

Each serving provides:

195	Calories	37 g	Carbohydrate
6 g	Protein	0 mg	Cholesterol
2 g	Fat	4 g	Dietary Fiber

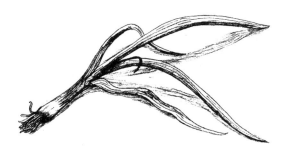

Shrimp, Vegetable, and Spaghetti Salad

Vegit is a seasoning found in the health-food sections of grocery stores.

Makes 4 servings

6 ounces spaghetti
1/2 pound asparagus, cut in 1-inch dice (use only the top
    4 inches of stalk)
1 carrot, sliced thinly on the diagonal
1/2 sweet red pepper, cut julienne
2 green onions, sliced thin
3 ounces mushrooms, sliced thin
1/3 cup defatted chicken stock
1 teaspoon vegetable seasoning (such as Vegit)
1 pound shrimp, peeled and deveined
2 teaspoons sesame oil
3 cloves garlic, minced
juice of 1 lemon
salt and pepper to taste
1/8 teaspoon chili paste or to taste
1/2 teaspoon grated fresh ginger
1 teaspoon soy sauce
1 teaspoon sugar
1/4 cup rice vinegar
1/2 cup orange juice
1 head radicchio

Cook spaghetti according to package directions. Rinse in cold
water, drain, and set aside.

Cook asparagus, carrot, red pepper, green onion, mush-rooms, and broth in a wok until liquid evaporates. Sprinkle with vegetable seasoning. Remove vegetables from wok and set aside.

Using a sharp knife, cut shrimp along the back where the vein was, almost through to the other side. Pull open to make a plumper-looking shrimp. Sauté shrimp in wok with 1 teaspoon of the sesame oil, garlic, and lemon juice until shrimp just turn pink. Season with salt and pepper to taste.

Combine vegetables, shrimp, and spaghetti in a large bowl and toss.

To make dressing, whisk together the remaining teaspoon of sesame oil, chili paste, ginger, soy sauce, sugar, vinegar and orange juice. Pour over salad and toss. Check seasoning and correct if necessary. Refrigerate at least 1 hour before serving. Line each plate with a large radicchio leaf. Place salad on top of leaf.

❖

Each serving provides:

327	Calories	46 g	Carbohydrate
27 g	Protein	173 mg	Cholesterol
4 g	Fat	3 g	Dietary Fiber

5

Pasta
Side Dishes

Vegetables Layered in Tomato Lasagna

If you are not making fresh pasta, try store-bought accordian squares. They look beautiful when the lasagna is cut.

Makes 9 side-dish servings

1/2 pound Tomato Pasta (page 17) or 1/2 pound lasagna
   noodles, cooked to package directions

Vegetable Filling

   1/2 onion, chopped
   1 cup sliced mushrooms
   2 zucchini, diced small
   1 cup broccoli flowerets
   1 pound spinach, chopped
   2 carrots, grated
   1/2 cup vegetable broth
   1 cup nonfat ricotta cheese
   salt and pepper to taste

Sauce

   1 can (28 ounces) tomato sauce
   1 1/2 cups vegetable broth
   1/2 cup dry white wine
   1/3 cup chopped fresh basil
   salt and pepper to taste

2 tablespoons freshly grated mozzarella or Parmesan cheese
   (optional)

Make pasta dough. Roll out pasta to 1/8-inch thickness and cut into 3 × 4-inch rectangles. Set noodles aside on tea towels dusted with rice flour while making the filling and sauce.

Preheat oven to 350 degrees.

To make the filling, sauté onion for 1 minute in a pan that has been sprayed with olive oil spray. Add mushrooms, zucchini, broccoli, spinach, carrots, and 1/2 cup broth. Cook until liquid evaporates. Remove vegetables to a bowl. Add ricotta cheese and blend well. Season with salt and pepper to taste. Set aside.

To make the sauce, combine tomato sauce, 1 1/2 cups broth, wine, basil, and salt and pepper to taste in a saucepan. Cook, uncovered, over medium heat for 20 minutes. Set aside.

Boil 1 quart water in a large pot. Dip lasagna noodles in boiling water for 1 minute. Remove and drain. In a lasagna pan, spread 1/2 cup of the sauce on the bottom of the pan. Place one layer of lasagna noodles over the sauce. Spread half of the vegetable filling evenly over the noodles. Cover lightly with some of the sauce and then another layer of noodles. Spread the other half of the vegetable filling evenly on top. Cover again with sauce and then another layer of noodles. Spread remaining sauce on top of noodles. Sprinkle with cheese, if using, and cover. (The lasagna can be refrigerated overnight until ready to cook.) Bake for 30 minutes. Remove cover and bake 20 minutes more, until lasagna is bubbling and browned on the top.

Each serving provides:			
152	Calories	28 g	Carbohydrate
10 g	Protein	21 mg	Cholesterol
1 g	Fat	4 g	Dietary Fiber

Hot and Spicy Pasta with Tomato Mint Sauce

Add chicken or meat to this recipe for a delectable main dish.

Makes 4 side-dish servings

8 ounces Fire-Roasted Red Pepper Pasta with 1 to 2 teaspoons
 chili oil added, cut into pappardelle (page 16)
5 medium tomatoes
1 yellow onion
$^1/_2$ cup dry red wine
$^1/_4$ to $^1/_3$ cup tomato juice (use if tomatoes are not juicy)
$^1/_4$ cup chopped fresh mint (reserve 1 tablespoon for garnish)
salt and freshly ground pepper to taste
pecorino cheese shavings for garnish

Make pasta and let dry while making sauce.

 Spray a grill with vegetable spray and, over hot coals, grill tomatoes and onion until partially blackened. Peel and purée tomatoes. Chop the onion. Put both into a saucepan and add wine, tomato juice (if necessary), mint, salt, and pepper and cook, uncovered, over medium heat for 15 minutes to blend flavors.

Cook pasta until al dente, drain, and toss with sauce. Sprinkle with reserved tablespoon of mint and cheese.

Each serving provides:

204	Calories	37 g	Carbohydrate
7 g	Protein	38 mg	Cholesterol
3 g	Fat	4 g	Dietary Fiber

Sundried Tomato Pesto on Pasta

Makes 8 side-dish servings or 4 main-dish servings

8 ounces fusilli
3/4 cup lite evaporated milk
3 tablespoons Sundried Tomato Pesto (recipe follows)
1 tablespoon strained nonfat yogurt (page 10)
salt and pepper to taste
2 tablespoons pine nuts
freshly grated Romano cheese for garnish
chopped flat leaf parsley for garnish

Prepare pasta according to package directions. Drain and place in a large bowl. While pasta is cooking, stir evaporated milk, pesto, and yogurt together in a saucepan until well blended. Warm over low heat. Season with salt and pepper to taste.

Mix pine nuts with pasta. Toss sauce with pasta and pine nuts and sprinkle with Romano and parsley.

Each side-dish serving provides:

153	Calories	25 g	Carbohydrate
6 g	Protein	1 mg	Cholesterol
4 g	Fat	2 g	Dietary Fiber

Sundried Tomato Pesto

The sundried tomatoes make for an earthy-tasting pesto. This recipe makes more pesto than you need for the sauce, but the leftovers are sensational on sandwiches, pizzas, or mixed into guacamole. Spread some on crostini for a delicious treat.

1 cup sundried tomatoes soaked in 1/2 cup tomato juice until
    softened
2 tablespoons virgin olive oil
4 cloves garlic, minced
3 tablespoons freshly grated Romano cheese
1/4 cup pine nuts

Squeeze the liquid from the tomatoes and reserve. Purée tomatoes in a food processor. Add oil, garlic, cheese, and pine nuts and process until finely ground. Add reserved juice and process until well mixed. Store in covered container in refrigerator.

Each one-tablespoon serving provides:

63	Calories	4 g	Carbohydrate
2 g	Protein	1 mg	Cholesterol
5 g	Fat	1 g	Dietary Fiber

Pasta-Stuffed Mushrooms

This filling can also be used to stuff zucchini or cabbage leaves.

Makes 24 mushrooms

6 ounces orzo, cooked
3 cloves garlic, minced
2 shallots, minced
2 teaspoons virgin olive oil
10 ounces frozen chopped spinach, defrosted and squeezed dry
2 small zucchini, shredded
1/4 cup freshly grated Parmesan cheese
1 teaspoon dried thyme leaves
1 teaspoon dried oregano
2 tablespoons pine nuts
1/2 cup egg substitute
salt and pepper to taste
24 extra-large mushrooms

Preheat oven to 375 degrees.

Put orzo into a large bowl and set aside. Sauté the garlic and shallots in olive oil for 1 minute. Add the spinach and zucchini and cook for 2 minutes. Drain the spinach mixture and then stir into orzo. Add Parmesan, thyme, oregano, pine nuts, egg substitute, salt, and pepper and mix well.

Wipe off mushrooms with a damp cloth to remove dirt. Snap the stems out of the mushrooms and save for another use, such as soup stock.

Pasta with Peppers

A very colorful side dish.

Makes 4 side-dish servings

1 sweet red pepper, slivered
1 sweet yellow pepper, slivered
1 1/4 cups defatted chicken broth
1/2 onion, slivered
1 teaspoon butter
1/4 cup vermouth
1/2 to 1 teaspoon chili sauce
1 tablespoon chopped fresh tarragon
1 tablespoon chopped fresh parsley
2 teaspoons arrowroot mixed with 2 tablespoons water
salt and pepper to taste
4 ounces fusilli

Sauté red and yellow peppers in a nonstick pan with 1/4 cup of the broth until liquid evaporates. Add onion, 2 more tablespoons of the broth, butter, and cook again until liquid evaporates. Add remaining broth, vermouth, chile sauce, tarragon, and parsley and cook 2 minutes more. Remove from heat and

Fill each mushroom cap with the orzo filling, forming
mound. Put the mushrooms on a rimmed cookie sheet t
been sprayed with vegetable spray. Bake for 15 to 20 mi
or until firm to the touch.

❖

Each stuffed mushroom provides:

51	Calories	8 g	Carbohy
3 g	Protein	1 mg	Cholester
1 g	Fat	1 g	Dietary F

stir in arrowroot mixture. Place over low heat and continue stirring until thickened. Season with salt and pepper to taste.

Meanwhile, bring water to a boil, cook pasta al dente, and drain. Place in a large bowl. Pour sauce over pasta and toss well.

Each serving provides:

154	Calories	29 g	Carbohydrate
5 g	Protein	3 mg	Cholesterol
2 g	Fat	3 g	Dietary Fiber

Angel Hair Timbale
with Spinach Cream Sauce

I love to serve this for a first course at summer dinner parties.

Makes 8 side-dish servings

Angel Hair Timbale
>   dry unseasoned bread crumbs
>   4 ounces angel hair pasta (2 cups cooked)
>   1/2 cup minced onion
>   1/2 cup chopped mushrooms
>   1/4 cup defatted chicken broth
>   1/3 cup chopped fresh parsley
>   1/2 cup lowfat ricotta cheese
>   1/4 cup freshly grated Parmesan cheese
>   3 ounces Canadian bacon, minced
>   1 1/2 tablespoons minced fresh sage
>   3/4 cup egg substitute
>   3/4 cup lite evaporated milk
>   salt and pepper to taste

Spinach Cream Sauce
>   2 cups coarsely chopped spinach
>   1/4 cup minced onion
>   1/2 cup defatted chicken broth
>   1 cup lite evaporated milk mixed with 1 tablespoon
>   cornstarch
>   pinch of nutmeg
>   3 tablespoons nonfat sour cream
>   salt and white pepper to taste

freshly grated Romano cheese for garnish

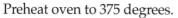

Preheat oven to 375 degrees.

Ready 8 ramekins for timbales: Cut out wax paper into rounds that just fit in the bottom of the ramekins. Spray ramekins with vegetable oil spray and insert wax paper rounds. Spray rounds with vegetable spray and sprinkle with the bread crumbs. Set aside.

Cook pasta until al dente, drain, and put into a large bowl.

Sauté onion and mushrooms in 1/4 cup broth until liquid evaporates. Add to pasta. Mix parsley, ricotta, Parmesan, Canadian bacon, sage, egg substitute, milk, salt, and pepper with pasta.

Fill each ramekin with a portion of the pasta mixture, pressing down to fit tightly. Put ramekins in a roasting pan. Fill pan with hot water halfway up the sides of the ramekins. Set a sheet of buttered wax paper over the ramekins. Bake for 50 to 60 minutes, or until firm when touched. Remove and let sit while you make the sauce.

To make the sauce, put spinach and onion into a pan with 1/2 cup broth and cook until liquid evaporates. Remove pan from heat. Add evaporated milk mixture and blend until smooth. Return to low heat. Add nutmeg and cook, stirring, until mixture thickens. Remove from heat and stir in sour cream and salt and pepper to taste.

To serve, ladle sauce onto plates and turn out a timbale on each. Drizzle top with sauce and garnish with grated cheese.

Each serving provides:

179	Calories	23 g	Carbohydrate
16 g	Protein	15 mg	Cholesterol
3 g	Fat	1 g	Dietary Fiber

Bows with Wild Mushroom Sauce

Wild mushrooms are available fresh almost everywhere now, but if you can't find them in your market, buy dried and reconstitute in warm water.

Makes 4 side-dish servings

1 ounce *each* morel, porcini, and chanterelle mushrooms, sliced
3 cloves garlic, chopped
2 teaspoons butter
2 tablespoons chopped fresh chives
1 tablespoon chopped fresh thyme
1 1/2 cups defatted beef broth
1/2 cup lite evaporated milk
1/4 cup nonfat sour cream
2 tablespoons chopped fresh parsley
salt and pepper to taste
8 ounces bow-shaped pasta

Sauté mushrooms in a nonstick pan with garlic and butter for 3 minutes. Add chives, thyme, and broth and simmer until liquid is reduced to 1/2 cup. Remove from heat and stir in milk, sour cream, parsley, and salt and pepper to taste. Blend well and warm over low heat.

Cook pasta according to package directions and drain. Toss with sauce and serve.

❖

Each serving provides:			
263	Calories	47 g	Carbohydrate
12 g	Protein	7 mg	Cholesterol
3 g	Fat	4 g	Dietary Fiber

Tomato Pasta with Onions and Spinach

Feta cheese is so flavorful that just a little lends terrific flavor.

Makes 8 side-dish servings

8 ounces Tomato Pasta, cut into fettuccine (page 17)
2 medium onions, chopped
1 cup chopped celery
1/2 cup chopped carrot
1 tablespoon chopped fresh lemon thyme
3 tablespoons chopped fresh parsley
1/2 cup dry white wine
1 3/4 cups defatted beef broth
1/2 pound spinach, slivered
1 tablespoon cornstarch
1/4 cup pine nuts
salt and pepper to taste
1/4 cup crumbled feta cheese
1 tablespoons minced fresh chives

Make pasta noodles and set aside to dry while preparing the sauce.

Put onions, celery, carrot, lemon thyme, parsley, wine, and 1 1/2 cups of the broth into a pan. Cook, uncovered, over medium heat for 20 minutes. Add spinach and cook 5 minutes more.

Mix the remaining 1/4 cup broth with 1 tablespoon cornstarch. Remove pan from heat and add cornstarch mixture, stirring until well blended. Return to low heat and continue cooking until slightly thickened. Stir in pine nuts and salt and pepper to taste.

Meanwhile, bring water to a boil, add pasta, and cook until al dente. Drain and place in a large serving bowl. Pour sauce over pasta and toss well. Sprinkle with feta and chives.

Each serving provides:

142	Calories	21 g	Carbohydrate
6 g	Protein	22 mg	Cholesterol
4 g	Fat	3 g	Dietary Fiber

6

Pasta with Vegetables

Broccoli aNd Pasta iN Cauliflower Curry Sauce

Start out with the smaller amount of curry paste and add more as you like, tasting as you go, so the dish is not too spicy. Puréed cauliflower is a wonderful thickener for sauces and soups — as you will see in this recipe.

Makes 6 servings

$1/4$ cup slivered almonds (reserve 1 tablespoon for garnish)
3 cups broccoli flowerets
2 tomatoes, each cut into 8 wedges
$1/4$ cup slivered fresh basil (reserve 1 tablespoon for garnish)
1 cup cauliflower flowerets
$2 1/2$ cups defatted chicken broth
1 to 3 teaspoons yellow curry paste to taste
1 teaspoon coriander seeds, crushed
$1/3$ cup dry white wine
salt and pepper to taste
12 ounces bow-shaped pasta

Toast almonds in a nonstick pan over medium heat, shaking the pan, until they just begin to turn brown.

Blanch broccoli and mix with almonds, tomatoes, and basil and set aside. Cook cauliflower in broth until very tender and soft. Remove cauliflower, leaving broth in pan, and purée. Put puréed cauliflower back into saucepan with broth. Stir in curry paste, coriander, wine, and salt and pepper to taste. Cook, stirring to blend flavors, for 2 minutes. Stir in broccoli mixture and coat with sauce. Warm thoroughly, but do not overcook. (You just want to warm the tomatoes, not cook them.)

Meanwhile, bring water to a boil, add pasta, and cook until al dente. Drain and place in a large bowl. Pour sauce over pasta and garnish with reserved basil and almonds.

Each serving provides:

276	Calories	50 g	Carbohydrate
12 g	Protein	0 mg	Cholesterol
3 g	Fat	8 g	Dietary Fiber

TOMATO PASTA WITH
ASPARAGUS AND MUSHROOMS

Try adding chicken or veal to this dish — it makes a delicious, yet still light, meal.

Makes 6 servings

12 ounces Tomato Pasta, cut into angel hair (page 17)
2 cloves garlic, minced
1 1/2 cups sliced mushrooms
1 small carrot, shredded
1/4 teaspoon red pepper flakes
2 teaspoons virgin olive oil
2 cups asparagus tips
1 tablespoon minced fresh tarragon
2 teaspoons chopped fresh thyme
2 cups defatted chicken broth or vegetable broth
1/4 cup sliced green onions
2 teaspoons dry sherry
1/2 cup strained nonfat yogurt (page 10)
salt and pepper to taste
freshly grated Romano cheese

Make pasta and set noodles aside to dry while making the sauce.

Put garlic, mushrooms, carrot, pepper flakes, and olive oil in a pan and cook until liquid released from mushrooms evaporates. Add asparagus, tarragon, thyme, and 1/2 cup of the broth and cook until liquid evaporates or asparagus is tender. Add remaining 1 1/2 cups broth, green onions, and sherry and cook 1 minute more. Remove from heat and set aside.

Meanwhile, bring water to a boil, add pasta, and cook until al dente. Drain pasta and place in a warmed large serving bowl. Stir yogurt into slightly cooled sauce until well blended. Season with salt and pepper to taste. Warm over very low heat, if necessary, and pour over pasta and toss. Serve with the Romano.

❖

Each serving provides:

216	Calories	35 g	Carbohydrate
10 g	Protein	41 mg	Cholesterol
4 g	Fat	2 g	Dietary Fiber

Fusilli with Green Vegetables in Chèvre-Walnut Sauce

Change the vegetables to suit your taste.

Makes 6 servings

2 tablespoons walnut pieces
1 cup broccoli flowerets
$^1/_2$ cup asparagus tips
$^1/_2$ cup green beans, cut on the diagonal into 1-inch pieces
2 celery stalks, sliced thinly on the diagonal
1 cup shredded cabbage
1 $^1/_2$ cups defatted chicken broth or vegetable broth
1 cup nonfat milk
2 tablespoons dry sherry
1 $^1/_2$ ounces chèvre
1 teaspoon white pepper
salt to taste
12 ounces fusilli or other corkscrew pasta
freshly grated Parmesan cheese

Toast walnuts in a nonstick pan over medium heat, shaking the pan, until they just begin to turn brown. Remove walnuts from pan, mince, and set aside. Steam broccoli, asparagus, green beans, and celery to desired tenderness. Set aside in a large bowl.

Cook cabbage in broth until soft. Strain cabbage, reserving the broth, and purée. Return broth to pan. Add the puréed

❖

cabbage, milk, sherry, and chèvre, and cook, stirring, until smooth. Stir in walnuts, white pepper, and salt.

Meanwhile, bring water to a boil, add pasta and cook until al dente. Drain and toss with vegetables. Turn all into pan with sauce and mix well. Serve with Parmesan.

❖

Each serving provides:

285	Calories	48 g	Carbohydrate
13 g	Protein	5 mg	Cholesterol
4 g	Fat	6 g	Dietary Fiber

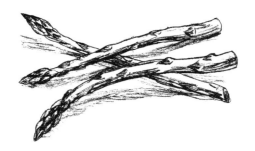

Pesto Cannelloni with Vegetables in Pepper Cream Sauce

Makes 6 servings

Pesto Pasta

　　2 cups all-purpose unbleached flour

　　2 tablespoons Pesto Sauce (page 29)

　　$3/4$ cup egg substitute

　　1 tablespoon water

　　1 teaspoon salt

Vegetable Filling

　　1 onion, chopped

　　2 cups chopped asparagus

　　1 large sweet red pepper, chopped

　　1 cup sliced mushrooms

　　1 cup chopped cauliflower

　　1 cup chopped broccoli

　　$1/4$ cup vegetable broth

　　$1 1/2$ teaspoons dried tarragon

　　1 tablespoons chopped fresh parsley

　　$1/2$ teaspoon pepper

Pepper Cream Sauce

　　3 fire-roasted red peppers, puréed

　　$2 3/4$ cups vegetable broth

　　salt and pepper to taste

　　$1/2$ cup nonfat milk mixed with 1 tablespoon flour

6 ounces shredded nonfat mozzarella cheese

Preheat oven to 350 degrees. Spray a large baking dish with vegetable spray.

Make pasta dough as described on page 2 in the Introduction. After dough has rested, divide into 10 pieces and shape each into a ball. Roll out each dough ball into a circle about 1/8 inch thick. Spread circles of dough out on clean tea towel or cookie sheets dusted with rice flour and let dry for at least 1 hour.

To make the filling, cook onion, asparagus, red pepper, mushrooms, cauliflower, and broccoli in 1/4 cup broth until liquid evaporates. Mix in tarragon, parsley, and pepper. Set aside.

To make the sauce, put fire-roasted peppers, 2 3/4 cups broth, salt, and pepper into a saucepan and cook, uncovered, over low heat until blended. Remove from the heat and stir in the milk mixture. Return to very low heat and cook, stirring, until sauce begins to thicken slightly.

Put 1 cup of the sauce on the bottom of the prepared baking dish.

In a 10-inch skillet filled halfway with boiling water, cook 1 pasta circle for 1 minute.Remove with a large slotted spoon and let water drain off. Fill as described before cooking the rest of the noodles. Place pasta circle on a plate and put approximately 3 tablespoons of the filling down the center of the noodle. Roll up pasta circle as you would a crepe and place in baking dish, seam side down. Continue until all the filling is used. Pour remaining sauce over cannelloni and sprinkle with mozarella. Cover with foil. Bake for 30 minutes. Uncover and cook 10 minutes more, until bubbling. Let stand 5 minutes before serving.

Each serving provides:

298	Calories	50 g	Carbohydrate
21 g	Protein	6 mg	Cholesterol
2 g	Fat	4 g	Dietary Fiber

Tri-Colored Lasagna with Vegetables

You will be using just a little of each of these pastas for the lasagna. With the leftover dough, one suggestion is to cut it into fettuccine and make a colorful pasta salad or primavera. This recipe is a lot of work, but for a special occasion, it is worth making for the accolades you will receive.

Makes 12 servings

1 recipe Tomato Pasta (page 17)
1 recipe Spinach Pasta (page 17)
1 recipe Basic Egg Pasta (page 15)

Sauce

    3 ounces feta cheese, crumbled
    5 cups White Cream Sauce No. 1 or No. 2 (page 32 or 33)

Mushroom Filling

    2 cups chopped wild mushrooms
    1 cup minced onion
    2 tablespoons vegetable broth
    1/2 cup lowfat cottage cheese
    1 teaspoon dried thyme leaves
    3 tablespoons egg substitute
    salt and pepper to taste

Red Pepper Filling

    4 red peppers, diced
    1/3 cup lowfat cottage cheese
    1 teaspoon dried basil
    3 tablespoons egg substitute
    salt and pepper to taste

Broccoli Filling
>   3 cups chopped broccoli, blanched
>   1/3 cup lowfat cottage cheese
>   1 teaspoon dried basil
>   3 tablespoons egg substitute
>   salt and pepper to taste

Make pasta doughs. Roll out about one-third of each type dough. Cut 4 lasagna noodles (3×4-inch rectangles) of each type. Let dry for 20 to 30 minutes on clean tea towels or cookie sheets sprinkled with rice flour.

Meanwhile, blend feta cheese into the white sauce. Set aside.

Preheat oven to 375 degrees. Spray a 9×13-inch baking pan with vegetable spray.

To make the mushroom filling, cook the mushrooms and onion in the broth until liquid evaporates. Remove pan from the heat. Blend in the cottage cheese, thyme, egg substitute, and salt and pepper to taste. Set aside.

To make the red pepper filling, sauté the red peppers in a pan that has been sprayed with vegetable spray for 1 minute. Remove peppers from pan, drain, and place in a bowl. Add cottage cheese, basil, egg substitute, salt, and pepper to bowl and mix well. Set aside.

To make the broccoli filling, mix the broccoli with the cottage cheese, basil, egg sustitute, salt, and pepper. Set aside.

Cook 4 tomato lasagna noodles in boiling water until al dente. Drain and lay 3 of the noodles in the bottom of pan. Spread the mushroom filling evenly over first layer of noodles. Pour 1 cup of the white sauce over the filling.

Cook 4 spinach noodles until al dente. Drain and lay 3 of the noodles over mushroom filling. Spread the red pepper filling evenly over the spinach noodles. Cover with 1 cup of the white sauce.

Cook 4 egg lasagna noodles until al dente, drain, and lay 3 of the noodles on top of the red pepper filling. Spread the broccoli filling evenly over the egg noodles. Cover with 1 cup of the white sauce.

Lay 1 noodle of each color pasta on top of the broccoli filling. Cover with the remaining white sauce. Cover and bake for 30 minutes, until bubbling and browned. Remove from oven and let stand 10 minutes before serving.

❖

Each serving provides:

261	Calories	40 g	Carbohydrate
15 g	Protein	66 mg	Cholesterol
4 g	Fat	3 g	Dietary Fiber

Spaghetti with Peas and Peppers

Gorgonzola cheese, when slowly melted, makes a savory, smooth sauce.

Makes 6 servings

1/2 cup chopped onion
1/2 cup *each* slivered sweet yellow, red, and green peppers
1/2 cup slivered kale
1 cup fresh or frozen peas
3/4 cup vegetable broth
2 cups Mushroom Sauce (page 30)
4 ounces Gorgonzola cheese
10 ounces spaghetti
chopped fresh parsley for garnish

Put onion, peppers, kale, peas, and broth in a nonstick pan and cook until liquid evaporates. Set aside.

Warm the Mushroom Sauce and stir in Gorgonzola cheese, mashing cheese in pan, until sauce is smooth. Stir vegetables into sauce.

Meanwhile, bring water to a boil, add pasta, and cook until al dente. Drain and place in a large serving bowl. Pour sauce over pasta and toss well. Sprinkle with parsley and serve.

	Each serving provides:		
408	Calories	68 g	Carbohydrate
17 g	Protein	17 mg	Cholesterol
7 g	Fat	4 g	Dietary Fiber

Mélange of Seasonal Vegetables with Black Pepper Fettuccine

For best-tasting results, use vegetables that are in season.

Makes 8 servings

1 pound Black Pepper Pasta, cut in fettuccine (page 15)
$1/2$ cup asparagus tips
$1/3$ cup fresh peas
1 cup green beans, cut in 1-inch pieces
1 small sweet red pepper, slivered
1 carrot, cut julienne
2 small zucchini, cut julienne
3 cloves garlic, minced
2 $1/2$ cups vegetable broth
10 yellow pear tomatoes, cut in half if large
3 green onions, sliced
1 tablespoon chopped fresh dill
2 teaspoons chopped lemon thyme
$1/3$ cup white wine mixed with 1 tablespoon cornstarch
salt and pepper to taste
2 tablespoons freshly grated Asiago cheese for garnish
2 tablespoons chopped fresh parsley for garnish

Make pasta noodles and set aside to dry while preparing the vegetables.

Put asparagus, peas, green beans, red pepper, carrot, zucchini, garlic, and $1/2$ cup of the broth into a nonstick wok and cook, uncovered, until liquid evaporates. Add the remaining 2 cups broth, tomatoes, green onions, dill, thyme, and heat through. Remove pan from heat and add the wine mixture. Cook over very low heat until mixture begins to thicken. Season with salt and pepper to taste.

Meanwhile, bring water to a boil, add pasta, and cook until al dente. Drain and toss with vegetables. Garnish with cheese and parsley.

Each serving provides:

216	Calories	36 g	Carbohydrate
9 g	Protein	98 mg	Cholesterol
4 g	Fat	2 g	Dietary Fiber

Sweet Potato Fettuccine with Chanterelles in Chèvre Sauce

Makes 4 servings

8 ounces Sweet Potato Pasta, cut in fettuccine (page 17)

2 teaspoons virgin olive oil

3 shallots, chopped

2 tablespoons chopped fresh thyme or 2 teaspoons dried thyme leaves

1 pound chanterelle mushrooms, sliced

1/2 cup chardonnay wine

3 ounces chèvre, crumbled

1 1/4 cup defatted chicken broth

pinch of cayenne pepper

1/2 cup lite evaporated milk mixed with 1 1/2 tablespoons cornstarch

1 tablespoon chopped parsley

Make pasta noodles and set aside to dry while preparing mushrooms and sauce.

Put olive oil, shallots, 1 tablespoon of the thyme, and chanterelles into a nonstick pan and cook, stirring, until shallots are transparent. Add wine and cook 3 minutes more. Add chèvre and blend well. Add broth and cayenne and cook, stirring, over low heat to totally incorporate the chèvre. Remove from the heat and stir in cornstarch mixture. When well blended, put on low heat, stirring in last tablespoon of the thyme and the parsley, until mixture thickens.

Meanwhile, bring water to a boil, add pasta, and cook until al dente. Drain and place in a large serving bowl. Pour sauce over noodles and toss.

Each serving provides:

321	Calories	43 g	Carbohydrate
15 g	Protein	49 mg	Cholesterol
9 g	Fat	3 g	Dietary Fiber

Basil Cannelloni with Peppers and Zucchini

You can use charred red peppers that are bottled in water or blacken fresh peppers over gas heat on the stove, on the grill, or under the broiler. Turn until peppers are black and blistery all over. Immediately put into a plastic bag, seal, and let sit 10 minutes. Remove from bag and with the edge of a knife, remove skin, seeds, and core.

Makes 6 servings

1 recipe Basil and Garlic Pasta (page 15)

Zucchini Filling
>   2 green zucchini, shredded
>   2 yellow zucchini, shredded
>   4 ounces mushrooms, chopped
>   1 carrot, grated
>   3 green onions, diced
>   2 teaspoons virgin olive oil
>   3 tablespoons dry unseasoned bread crumbs
>   1 1/2 teaspoons fennel seed
>   salt and pepper to taste
>   1 egg white

Pepper Sauce
>   2 red peppers, roasted, peeled, and diced (or 1 jar
>   (6 ounces) fire-roasted red peppers)
>   1 cup lowfat cottage cheese
>   1/4 cup lowfat sour cream
>   1 cup defatted chicken broth
>   salt and pepper to taste
>   1 tablespoon freshly grated Romano cheese

Make pasta dough. After dough has rested, roll out to ¹/₈-inch thickness and cut into 4 × 4-inch squares. Drop squares of dough into boiling water for 1 minute. Remove and put into cold water. Drain squares of dough as needed.

Preheat oven to 400 degrees.

To make the filling, put zucchini, mushrooms, carrot, green onions, and olive oil into a pan and cook over medium heat until liquid from vegetables evaporates. Remove pan from the heat. Stir in bread crumbs, fennel seed, salt, pepper, and egg white. Mix well and set aside.

To make sauce, purée roasted peppers. Purée cottage cheese until smooth and mix with pepper purée. Stir in sour cream and broth and season with salt and pepper. Set aside.

To assemble, place 2 tablespoons of the filling down the center of a pasta square and roll up like a crepe. Place seam side down in a baking dish sprayed with vegetable spray and continue until all cannelloni are filled.

Ladle sauce over cannelloni and sprinkle with cheese. Bake, uncovered, for about 20 minutes, until bubbling.

Each serving provides:

410	Calories	61 g	Carbohydrate
21 g	Protein	185 mg	Cholesterol
9 g	Fat	4 g	Dietary Fiber

Roasted Ratatouille on Rigatoni

Roasting the vegetables gives this dish a rich flavor with very little fat.

Makes 8 servings

1 sweet potato, peeled and diced
1 onion, peeled and cut into eighths
3 cloves garlic, peeled and left whole
1 carrot, diced
1 sweet red pepper, cut in half and seeded
1 sweet green pepper, cut in half and seeded
1 medium zucchini, diced
1 parsnip, peeled and diced
6 Italian plum tomatoes, peeled, seeded, and diced
1/4 cup chopped fresh basil
1 tablespoon chopped fresh thyme
1 bay leaf
2 tablespoons virgin olive oil
1 teaspoon coarsely cracked black pepper
1 tablespoon brown sugar
salt to taste
1 pound rigatoni
1/4 cup pecorino cheese shavings for garnish

Preheat oven to 375 degrees.

Put vegetables into a roasting pan that has been sprayed with vegetable spray. Sprinkle with basil, thyme, bay leaf, olive oil, pepper, and brown sugar. Toss together and bake, covered, for 30 minutes. Remove peppers, peel and dice. Return diced peppers to the pan and continue cooking the vegetables, uncovered, for 15 to 20 minutes more, or until vegetables are tender. Discard bay leaf. Season with salt to taste.

Meanwhile, bring water to a boil, add pasta, and cook until al dente. Drain and place in a serving bowl. Pour vegetables over rigatoni. Garnish with cheese.

Each serving provides:

301	Calories	56 g	Carbohydrate
9 g	Protein	1 mg	Cholesterol
5 g	Fat	7 g	Dietary Fiber

Bow Pasta with Tomatoes and Pine Nuts

On busy days, this quick and delicious pasta makes a satisfying meal.

Makes 4 servings

1/3 cup sliced green onion
4 cloves garlic, minced
2 large tomatoes, peeled, seeded, and diced
1 cup vegetable broth
1/4 to 1/2 teaspoon chili sauce or to taste
1/4 cup slivered fresh basil
2 tablespoons pine nuts
8 ounces bow-shaped pasta
1 1/2 tablespoons feta cheese, crumbled

Put onion, garlic, tomatoes, and 1/2 cup of the broth into a non-stick pan and cook on low heat until liquid evaporates. Add remaining 1/2 cup of the broth, chili sauce, basil, and pine nuts and cook 2 minutes more.

Meanwhile, bring water to a boil, add pasta, and cook until al dente. Drain and place in a large serving bowl. Pour sauce over pasta and toss. Sprinkle with cheese.

Each serving provides:

267	Calories	47 g	Carbohydrate
10 g	Protein	5 mg	Cholesterol
5 g	Fat	5 g	Dietary Fiber

7

Pasta
with Meat

Tagliatelle with Pork in Rosemary Whiskey Sauce

I like to cook with whiskey — it gives sauces a nice, rich flavor.

Makes 6 servings

1 pound pork tenderloin
3 teaspoons garlic paste
3 sprigs fresh rosemary
1 teaspoon coarsely ground black pepper
1 medium yellow zucchini, cut julienne
4 dried apricots, slivered
1 cup sliced mushrooms
1 3/4 cup defatted beef broth
1 teaspoon chopped fresh rosemary
2 tablespoons whiskey
salt and pepper to taste
2 tablespoons water mixed with 1 tablespoon cornstarch
10 ounces tagliatelle
snipped fresh chives for garnish

Preheat oven to 450 degrees.

Rub tenderloin with garlic paste, rosemary sprigs, and pepper. Put on a rack in a rimmed cookie sheet. Reduce heat to 375 degrees and cook for 30 to 40 minutes, or until desired doneness.

Cook zucchini, apricots, and mushrooms in 1/4 cup of the broth until liquid evaporates. Add remaining 1 1/2 cups broth, chopped rosemary, whiskey, salt, and pepper and cook, stirring, until well blended. Remove from heat and stir in cornstarch mixture. Return to heat and cook over low heat until thickened slightly.

Slice meat thinly and toss with sauce.

Meanwhile, bring water to a boil, add pasta, and cook until al dente. Drain and toss with meat and sauce. Serve garnished with fresh snipped chives.

Each serving provides:

322	Calories	46 g	Carbohydrate
24 g	Protein	53 mg	Cholesterol
4 g	Fat	4 g	Dietary Fiber

Baked Rigatoni and Ham in Wine Sauce

This dish can be assembled in the morning to be baked later that night for dinner.

Makes 8 servings

12 ounces rigatoni, cooked al dente and drained
6 ounces Canadian bacon, diced
2 cups tiny broccoli flowerets, blanched
3 tablespoons diced green chiles
6 ounces grated nonfat mozzarella cheese
1 cup lowfat cottage cheese
1/3 cup lowfat yogurt
1 cup defatted chicken broth
1/3 cup dry white wine
1/2 teaspoon dry mustard
1 teaspoon Worcestershire sauce
salt and pepper to taste
2 tablespoons dry unseasoned bread crumbs
2 tablespoons freshly grated Romano cheese

Preheat oven to 375 degrees.
  Spray a gratin dish with vegetable spray and set aside.
  Put rigatoni, Canadian bacon, broccoli, chiles, and mozzarella in a large bowl. Cream cottage cheese in a blender. Add yogurt, broth, wine, mustard, Worcestershire sauce, salt, and pepper and blend well. Mix into pasta mixture and turn into

prepared dish. Cover and cook for 20 minutes. Remove dish
from oven and uncover. Mix together bread crumbs and
cheese and sprinkle over baked pasta mixture. Return to oven,
uncovered, and bake another 10 minutes, or until lightly
browned.

Each serving provides:

281	Calories	37 g	Carbohydrate
24 g	Protein	20 mg	Cholesterol
4 g	Fat	4 g	Dietary Fiber

Manicotti with Wild Mushrooms and Beef

My mother made this dish using dried Italian mushrooms instead of wild mushrooms. Dried Italian mushrooms are very expensive in North America. My family was lucky to have an Italian friend that kept our supply stocked with her frequent visits to Italy. Store dried mushrooms with a couple tablespoons of peppercorns and a few bay leaves in a jar with a tight-fitting lid.

Makes 6 servings

1 recipe Basic Egg Pasta (page 15)

3 cups chopped assorted wild mushrooms (shiitake, chanterelle, or porcini)

2 leeks, white part only, diced

3 cloves garlic, chopped

1 carrot, minced

1 stalk celery, minced

$^1/_2$ cup defatted beef broth

$^1/_2$ pound round steak, all visible fat removed and ground or diced small

$^1/_2$ cup lowfat ricotta

1 teaspoon dried thyme leaves

$^1/_2$ teaspoon dried marjoram

2 tablespoons chopped flat leaf parsley

$^1/_4$ cup egg substitute

salt and pepper to taste

4 cups Light Tomato-Basil Sauce substituting thyme for the basil (page 28)

3 tablespoons freshly grated Asiago cheese

Make pasta dough. After dough has rested, roll out to 1/8-inch thickness and cut twelve 4 × 4-inch squares. Set aside to dry for 20 to 30 minutes on cookie sheets that have been sprinkled with rice flour.

Preheat oven to 375 degrees. Spray a 9 × 13-inch baking dish with vegetable spray and set aside.

Put mushrooms, leeks, garlic, carrot, and celery into a saucepan with broth and cook until liquid evaporates. Remove vegetables from pan and put into a bowl. Sauté beef in same pan until all pink is gone. Drain and add to bowl with vegetables. Stir in ricotta, thyme, marjoram, parsley, egg substitute, salt, and pepper. Blend well.

Put 1 cup of the tomato sauce in the bottom of the prepared baking dish. Boil 4 cups water in a flat fry pan or wok. Remove pan from heat. Dip 1 pasta square into the hot water for a few seconds. Drain and place on a plate to fill. Put about 1/4 cup of the filling and 1 tablespoon of the sauce down the center of the pasta square. Roll up like a crepe and put seam side down in the pan. Continue until all pasta is filled and put into baking dish. Pour rest of sauce over pasta and sprinkle with cheese. Cover and bake for 20 minutes. Uncover and bake 10 minutes more, until bubbling.

Each serving provides:

461	Calories	64 g	Carbohydrate
27 g	Protein	207 mg	Cholesterol
10 g	Fat	5 g	Dietary Fiber

Pappardelle and Pork in Orange and Green Onion Sauce

Garlic paste imported from Italy comes in a tube and is found in most grocery stores and gourmet shops. It lends a delicious flavor to roasts.

Makes 8 servings

1 pound Basic Egg Pasta, cut into pappardelle (page 15)
1 pound pork tenderloin, all visible fat removed
2 teaspoons garlic paste
1 teaspoon dried rosemary
1/3 cup frozen orange juice concentrate
2 teaspoons orange zest
1 teaspoon grated fresh ginger
1 tablespoon hoisin sauce
1 tablespoon soy sauce
4 green onions, sliced
1/2 cup defatted chicken broth
2 tablespoons Grand Marnier mixed with 3 teaspoons
    cornstarch
salt and pepper to taste

Preheat oven to 375 degrees.

Make pasta noodles and let dry while cooking pork and making sauce.

Rub entire pork tenderloin with garlic paste and sprinkle with rosemary. Put on a rack in a rimmed cookie sheet and cook for 45 minutes. Remove meat and cover with foil while making sauce.

Start water boiling for pasta. To make sauce, mix concentrate, zest, ginger, hoisin sauce, soy sauce, green onions, and broth in a saucepan and warm over low heat Add cornstarch mixture and continue warming until sauce just begins to thicken. Season with salt and pepper.

Cook pasta until al dente and drain. Slice pork very thinly and toss pasta and pork with sauce.

Each serving provides:

265	Calories	33 g	Carbohydrate
20 g	Protein	136 mg	Cholesterol
5 g	Fat	1 g	Dietary Fiber

Lasagna with Meat and Grilled Vegetables

Makes 12 servings

1 ½ pounds pork tenderloin, all visible fat removed
1 can (28 ounces) whole tomatoes, crushed
1 medium onion, minced
4 cloves garlic, minced
1 teaspoon chili powder
1 red pepper
1 bell pepper
2 zucchini
2 Japanese eggplants
2 ears of corn, husked
12 ounces lowfat ricotta cheese
8 ounces lowfat cottage cheese
1 pound lasagna noodles
4 cups Light Tomato-Basil Sauce, substituting cilantro for
    the basil (page 28)
⅓ cup freshly grated dry Jack cheese

Preheat oven to 375 degrees.

Put pork, tomatoes, onion, garlic, and chili powder in a casserole and cook for 1 hour 15 minutes. Remove from oven and let sit 15 minutes. Shred meat, place in a bowl, and add the sauce remaining in casserole. Set aside. Turn oven down to 350 degrees.

Cut peppers, zucchini, and eggplants in half. Spray with olive oil spray. Spray corn lightly with olive oil spray. Grill all vegetables until grill marks appear and vegetables are tender. As soon as peppers are blackened, remove immediately to a plastic bag and seal tightly. Let sit for 10 minutes. Remove peppers from bag, peel, and dice. Put into a large bowl. Dice up zucchini and eggplant and add to bowl. Cut corn off cob and add to bowl. Set aside.

Mix ricotta and cottage cheese. Set aside. Meanwhile, cook lasagna noodles according to package directions, plunge in cold water, and place on damp tea towels.

Spray a 9 × 13-inch baking dish with vegetable spray. Put 1/2 cup of the tomato sauce in the bottom of the dish. Place a layer of noodles on top of the sauce in dish. Spread half of the ricotta mixture evenly over the noodles then half of the the meat mixture, then half of the vegetables. Cover with one-third of the sauce. Repeat starting with noodles,then ricotta, meat, vegetables, and one-third of the sauce. Place a layer of noodles on top, then cover with the remaining sauce. Sprinkle top with cheese. Cover and bake for 20 minutes. Uncover and cook 10 to 15 minutes more, or until hot and bubbling.

Each serving provides:

332	Calories	43 g	Carbohydrate
27 g	Protein	50 mg	Cholesterol
6 g	Fat	3 g	Dietary Fiber

Spaghetti Carbonara

As a coordinator for foreign exchange students, I hosted a group of Italian students from Rome. One of our exchange students, Mirko, often made spaghetti carbonara for me. Many people add garlic, parsley, or onions to the traditional version of this dish, but Mirko says that is not the true Roman way. Of course, I have tampered with the original recipe to reduce the fat — something Mirko would not approve of!

Makes 4 servings

4 ounces Canadian bacon, diced
1 tablespoon virgin olive oil
8 ounces spaghetti
2 tablespoons lite evaporated milk
2 eggs, beaten
3 tablespoons freshly grated pecorino cheese

Cook Canadian bacon in olive oil over low heat while you cook the spaghetti in boiling water. Meanwhile, beat the evaporated milk, eggs, and cheese together until well mixed.

Drain the pasta and put into a bowl, adding the bacon in olive oil over the pasta. Quickly toss the egg mixture with the pasta and serve immediately. Pass around more cheese if desired.

Each serving provides:

362	Calories	47 g	Carbohydrate
20 g	Protein	127 mg	Cholesterol
10 g	Fat	3 g	Dietary Fiber

Potato-Leek Sauce on Fusilli

*My favorite soup on a cold winter day is potato leek, which inspired
me to create this delicious sauce.*

Makes 8 servings

2 leeks, white part only, sliced
1 teaspoon butter
3 1/2 cups defatted chicken broth
3 medium russet potatoes, peeled and diced
1/3 cup chopped celery
1/3 cup chopped carrot
1/3 cup minced sweet red pepper
3 ounces Canadian Bacon, diced small
1 pound fusilli
2 tablespoons freshly grated Parmesan cheese for garnish
1 tablespoon chopped flat leaf parsley for garnish

To make sauce, slowly sauté leeks in butter and 1/4 cup of the
broth until leeks are very soft. Add potatoes and 2 3/4 cups of
the broth and cook, covered, over medium heat 15 to 20 minutes, until potatoes are tender. Purée mixture and set aside.

Into same pan, put remaining 1/2 cup of the broth, celery,
carrot, red pepper, and Canadian bacon. Cook until liquid
evaporates.

Meanwhile bring water to a boil, add pasta, and cook until al dente. Drain and toss with vegetable mixture. Pour potato-leek sauce over all and blend. Serve garnished with cheese and parsley.

❖

Each serving provides:

285	Calories	53 g	Carbohydrate
12 g	Protein	9 mg	Cholesterol
3 g	Fat	5 g	Dietary Fiber

Rigatoni with Fillet Strips in Onion Broth

Long, slow cooking gives onions a lovely, sweet flavor, not to mention their delightful aroma.

Makes 4 servings

2 large onions, thinly sliced
6 cups defatted beef broth
2 cups water
1 tablespoon tomato paste
1 teaspoon dried thyme leaves
1 teaspoon dried marjoram
12 ounces beef fillet, all visible fat removed and cut into strips
salt and pepper to taste
8 ounces rigatoni
2 teaspoons chopped fresh parsley for garnish

To make the onion broth, put onions, broth, water, tomato paste, thyme, and marjoram into a nonstick soup pot and cook over low heat for 2 hours, covered. Set aside.

Start water boiling for the pasta while you cook the meat. Heat a heavy sauté pan to very hot and spray with butter-flavored vegetable spray. Sauté beef quickly until desired doneness. Remove meat and put into onion broth. Put about 1/2 cup of the onion broth into the sauté pan, and scrape the brown bits from the pan, mixing them with the broth. Pour this into onion broth with meat. Season with salt and pepper.

Cook pasta until al dente, drain, and mix in with beef mixture. Serve immediately and sprinkle with parsley.

Each serving provides:

389	Calories	48 g	Carbohydrate
30 g	Protein	57 mg	Cholesterol
8 g	Fat	5 g	Dietary Fiber

Lasagna with Beef and Hearty Chili Sauce

This dish promises to be a favorite with chili lovers everywhere. Adjust the hotness to your liking.

Makes 12 servings

1 pound pinto beans
1 1/2 pounds lean round steak
1 large onion, chopped
1 large sweet green pepper, chopped
3 whole tomatoes, peeled, seeded, and chopped
1 can (15 ounces) tomato sauce
1 cup catsup
1 cup water
3 tablespoons diced fresh jalapeño peppers
2 tablespoons Worcestershire sauce
1 tablespoon brown sugar
1 1/2 teaspoons cumin or to taste
1 teaspoon cayenne pepper or to taste
salt to taste
1 pound lasagna noodles
3/4 cup grated nonfat cheddar cheese
3/4 cup grated nonfat mozzarella cheese

Rinse and sort through beans. Cover with water and soak overnight.

Drain beans and put into a nonstick soup pot. Cover with fresh water. Add 2 quarts more water and cook for 2 hours.

Drain beans and return to pot. Add steak, onion, green pepper, tomatoes, tomato sauce, catsup, water, jalapeños, Worcestershire sauce, brown sugar, cumin, and cayenne. Cook, covered, over medium heat for 1 1/2 hours. Remove meat and shred. Set aside. Season chili with salt to taste and continue to cook until chili is quite thick, about 30 minutes more.

Preheat oven to 350°.

Meanwhile, bring water to a boil, add noodles, and cook until al dente. Plunge into cold water and drain as used. Spray a lasagna pan with vegetable spray and place a layer of noodles on the bottom. Spread with half of the shredded meat and then top with about one-third of the chili. Repeat process, starting and ending with noodles. Spread a thin layer of chili over the last noodle layer and then sprinkle top with cheeses. Bake, uncovered, 20 to 30 minutes, or until cheese is browned. Let lasagna sit for at least 10 minutes before serving.

❖

Each serving provides:

447	Calories	60 g	Carbohydrate
28 g	Protein	42 mg	Cholesterol
11 g	Fat	6 g	Dietary Fiber

Pasta Wheels and Steak in Creamy Thyme Sauce

Just smelling the irresistible aroma of my mother's meat sauce cooking made my mouth water. This dish brings me back to those times.

Makes 6 servings

2 cloves garlic, minced
1/2 cup finely chopped onion
3/4 pound lean sirloin, diced small
1/2 cup julienned green pepper
1/4 cup finely chopped celery
1/2 pound zucchini, diced small
1 can (28 ounces) whole peeled tomatoes, coarsely chopped
1/2 cup dry white wine
2 tablespoons chopped fresh thyme or 2 teaspoons dried
    thyme leaves
2 tablespoons chopped fresh parsley
1/2 cup lite evaporated milk
salt and pepper to taste
12 ounces pasta wheels
dried cheese curls, such as Parmesan, Asiago, or Romano
    for garnish

Sauté the garlic and onion in a nonstick pan sprayed with olive oil spray for 1 minute. Add meat and sauté until meat loses pink color. Add green pepper and celery and cook 2 more minutes. Add zucchini, tomatoes, wine, thyme, and parsley. Cook, uncovered, over medium heat until tomatoes cook down a bit and sauce slightly thickens, about 20 to 30 minutes. Remove sauce from heat and stir in evaporated milk and season with salt and pepper to taste.

Meanwhile, bring water to a boil, add pasta, and cook until al dente. Drain and toss with sauce. Garnish with cheese.

Each serving provides:

416	Calories	52 g	Carbohydrate
22 g	Protein	42 mg	Cholesterol
13 g	Fat	6 g	Dietary Fiber

Mushroom Pasta with Flank Steak in a Savory Broth

This dish is what home cooking is all about.

Makes 8 servings

³/₄ recipe of Mushroom Pasta, cut into pappardelle (page 16)
1 flank steak (1¹/₂ pounds)
2 teaspoons all-purpose unbleached flour
4 cups defatted beef broth
1 cup dry red wine
1 teaspoon sugar
1¹/₂ teaspoons dried thyme leaves
2 tablespoons chopped fresh parsley
salt and pepper to taste
2 tablespoons chopped fresh parsley for garnish

Make pasta and set aside.

Rub steak on both sides with flour. Brown steak in a nonstick pan sprayed with vegetable spray. Remove steak and add 3 cups of the broth, wine, sugar, thyme, and parsley to pan and blend well. Return steak to pan, cover, and cook for 50 minutes over medium heat. Turn steak once or twice during cooking and add water if necessary. When steak is done, remove from pan and add enough of the remaining broth to liquid left in the pan to make 2 cups. Let broth simmer while you thinly slice the meat. Season with salt and lots of pepper. Return sliced meat to broth while you cook the pasta.

Cook pasta until al dente and drain. To serve, put pasta on a platter and spoon meat over pasta. Pour more broth on top of pasta and garnish with parsley.

Each serving provides:

292	Calories	28 g	Carbohydrate
22 g	Protein	99 mg	Cholesterol
9 g	Fat	1 g	Dietary Fiber

Lemon Basil Fettuccine with Veal in Brandy Cream Sauce

You can find lemon-basil fettuccine in some supermarkets and in many gourmet food or houseware shops.

Makes 6 servings

1 pound veal, cut into 1/2-inch slices
juice of 1 lemon
2 teaspoons lemon zest
2 cloves garlic, minced
1 teaspoon unsalted butter
2/3 cup defatted beef broth
1/2 cup peeled and diced tomato
1 teaspoon dried thyme leaves
1 teaspoon sugar
1/2 cup slivered spinach leaves
12 ounces lite evaporated milk
1/4 cup nonfat sour cream
1/3 cup brandy
2 ounces Gorgonzola cheese
salt and pepper to taste
1 medium tomato, cored and cut into thin wedges
12 ounces lemon-basil fettuccine

Toss veal, lemon juice, lemon zest, and garlic together and let marinate for 10 minutes.

Spray a nonstick pan with butter-flavored vegetable spray and sauté veal in batches until done. Remove veal from pan.

Put butter, broth, diced tomato, thyme, sugar, and spinach into pan. Cook for 10 minutes over medium heat. Add meat and remove pan from stove. Stir in milk, sour cream, brandy, and cheese. Mash the cheese in the pan to blend well. Season with salt and pepper. Return pan to stove and warm over low heat. Add tomato wedges and let tomato just heat through.

Meanwhile, bring water to a boil, add pasta, and cook until al dente. Drain and toss with the sauce.

Each serving provides:

504	Calories	59 g	Carbohydrate
36 g	Protein	89 mg	Cholesterol
10 g	Fat	4 g	Dietary Fiber

Curry Pasta and Lamb in Champagne Sauce

Buy a good bottle of champagne to use in this recipe and enjoy the rest of the bubbly with your pasta.

Makes 6 servings

12 ounces Curry Pasta, cut into fettuccine (page 16)
1 pound lean lamb, cut into thin strips
3 tablespoons sliced green onion
3 cloves garlic, minced
2 teaspoons grated fresh ginger
1 cup defatted beef broth
1/2 cup champagne
1/2 cup lowfat coconut milk
1 teaspoon cinnamon
1 tablespoon brown sugar
2 tablespoons minced fresh mint
salt and pepper to taste
3 teaspoons cornstarch mixed with 2 tablespoons beef broth

Make pasta and set aside.

In a nonstick pan sprayed with butter-flavored vegetable spray, sauté meat until pink is almost gone. Put green onion, garlic, and ginger in with meat along with 1/4 cup of the broth. Cook until liquid evaporates. Add champagne, coconut milk, remaining 3/4 cup broth, cinnamon, brown sugar, and mint. Cook for 5 minutes or until meat is to desired doneness. Season with salt and pepper. Remove pan from heat and stir in corn-

❖

starch mixture. Return pan to stove and cook over very low heat, stirring, until sauce thickens.

Meanwhile, bring water to a boil, add pasta, and cook until al dente. Drain and pour sauce over pasta.

❖

Each serving provides:

320	Calories	32 g	Carbohydrate
25 g	Protein	75 mg	Cholesterol
8 g	Fat	1 g	Dietary Fiber

Mediterranean Cannelloni

For those who don't worry about sodium, you can add a tablespoon of anchovy paste to the sauce for an authentic Mediterranean flavor.

Makes 4 servings

8 cannelloni tubes

Filling

> $1/2$ pound lean sirloin, ground
> $1/2$ cup nonfat ricotta cheese
> $1/2$ cup chopped spinach, cooked and drained
> $1/3$ cup freshly grated Parmesan cheese
> salt and pepper to taste
> 2 egg whites

Sauce

> $1/2$ cup sliced green onion
> 2 cloves garlic, minced
> 4 large tomatoes, peeled, seeded, and chopped
> 1 cup tomato sauce
> $1/4$ teaspoon black pepper
> 2 tablespoons sliced black olives
> $1 1/2$ tablespoons drained tiny capers
> 1 teaspoon sugar
> $1/2$ cup dry white wine
> salt to taste

1 cup grated nonfat mozzarella cheese

Preheat oven to 375 degrees.

Partially cook cannelloni for five minutes according to package directions. Place in cold water until ready to fill.

To make the filling, sauté meat in a nonstick pan sprayed with vegetable spray until no pink appears. Set aside. Mix ricotta, spinach, Parmesan, salt, pepper, and egg whites. Add to meat and mix well. Set aside.

To make the sauce, put green onion and garlic in a nonstick pan sprayed with vegetable spray and sauté for 1 minute. Add tomatoes, tomato sauce, pepper, olives, capers, sugar, and wine. Cook mixture on low heat for 8 minutes. Season with salt to taste.

Drain cannelloni and stuff each with 1/4 cup of the filling. Lay each in a baking dish sprayed with vegetable spray. When all are stuffed and placed in dish, pour sauce over all and sprinkle with cheese. Cover and cook for 25 minutes. Remove cover and cook 10 to 15 minutes more, until bubbling.

Each serving provides:

490	Calories	56 g	Carbohydrate
30 g	Protein	51 mg	Cholesterol
15 g	Fat	7 g	Dietary Fiber

Mexican Lasagna with Cilantro Sauce

Slowly cooking the pork makes it shred beautifully and adds an authentic Mexican flavor.

Makes 8 servings

1 pound pork tenderloin
1 can (12 ounces) tomato sauce
$^1/_2$ cup water
1 teaspoon chili powder
2 tablespoons minced onion
1 can (4 ounces) diced green chiles, drained
2 tomatoes, peeled, seeded, and diced
3 tablespoons chopped fresh cilantro
1$^1/_2$ cups nonfat cottage cheese, drained
$^1/_2$ teaspoon *each* salt and pepper
1 pound lasagna noodles
4 cups White Cream Sauce No. 1 or No. 2, substituting
    the Parmesan with dry Jack cheese (page 32 or 33)
2 tablespoons dry Jack cheese

Preheat oven to 350 degrees.

Put pork, tomato sauce, water, chili powder, and onion in a small baking dish. Cover and cook for 1$^1/_2$ hours. Let cool. Remove pork and shred.Place pork in a large bowl and add the juices remaining in the baking dish. Stir in chiles, tomatoes, cilantro, cottage cheese, salt, and pepper.

Preheat oven to 375 degrees. Bring water to a boil, add noodles, and cook for 1 minute. Place in cold water, drain, and lay
on damp tea towels until ready to use.

Spray bottom of a 9 × 13-inch baking dish with olive oil
spray. Place a layer of noodles over bottom of pan. Spread half
of the pork mixture evenly over noodles and cover with 1 cup
of the white sauce. Layer again with noodles, cover with the
remaining pork mixture, and cover with another cup of the
white sauce. Top with noodles and 2 more cups of the white
sauce. Sprinkle with dry Jack cheese and bake, uncovered, for
20 to 25 minutes.

Each serving provides:

465	Calories	63 g	Carbohydrate
33 g	Protein	46 mg	Cholesterol
8 g	Fat	4 g	Dietary Fiber

Lasagna Layered with Meat, Vegetables, and Fennel Mashed Potatoes

After eating a mashed potato–topped pizza at a local parlor, I was inspired to create this lasagna. It is now a family favorite.

Makes 12 servings

Potato Filling

    3 large russet potatoes, peeled, cubed, and cooked
       until tender
    1 medium fennel bulb, chopped and cooked until tender
    1/4 cup nonfat milk
    salt and pepper to taste

Meat and Vegetable Filling

    1 1/2 pounds lean ground round (grind your own
       for less fat)
    1/2 cup finely chopped onion
    1/2 cup thinly sliced leek, white part only
    3 cloves garlic, minced
    1/2 cup thinly sliced carrots
    1/2 cup thinly sliced celery
    1 1/2 teaspoons dried sage leaves
    1 teaspoon dried thyme leaves
    1/2 cup vegetable broth

1 package (10 ounces) frozen chopped spinach, cooked
    and drained
$1/4$ cup egg substitute
salt and pepper to taste

1 pound lasagna noodles
4 cups White Cream Sauce No. 1 or No. 2 (page 32 or 33)
8 ounces shredded nonfat mozzarella cheese

Preheat oven to 350 degrees.

Mash the potatoes and purée the fennel. Mix the two together
and add as much of the milk as necessary to reach desired consistency. Season with salt and pepper to taste. Set aside.

Sauté the meat in a nonstick pan that has been sprayed with
olive oil spray. Break the meat up while it cooks, and continue
cooking until all pink is gone. Drain meat and remove to a
large bowl.

Into the same pan, put onions, leek, garlic, carrots, celery,
sage, thyme, and broth and cook until liquid evaporates. Transfer vegetables to bowl with the meat. Add spinach and egg
substitute and mix well. Season to taste with salt and pepper.
Set aside.

Cook lasagna noodles according to package directions,
drain, and put into cold water. Drain on damp tea towels.

Spray a 9 × 13-inch baking dish with olive oil spray and
put $1/2$ cup of the white sauce on the bottom. Place a layer of
noodles on top of the sauce. Spread a layer of the potato filling
on the noodles and then a layer of the meat and vegetable filling. Cover with $1/2$ cup of the white sauce. Repeat the process,
starting with a layer of noodles, then the potato filling, then the

meat filling, then the sauce. End with a layer of noodles. Pour the remaining sauce over all and sprinkle with the cheese.

Cover and cook for 30 minutes. Uncover and cook 10 to 15 minutes more or until top is nicely browned.

Each serving provides:

374	Calories	44 g	Carbohydrate
27 g	Protein	46 mg	Cholesterol
9 g	Fat	3 g	Dietary Fiber

8

Pasta with Fish

CRAB ROLL WITH CHAMPAGNE SAUCE

Wrapping this roll in cheesecloth helps the roll stay together while cooking so when it is unwrapped, it cuts beautifully.

Makes 6 servings

1 recipe Spinach Pasta or Saffron Pasta (page 17)
1 sweet red pepper, minced
1 small onion, minced
1 cup chopped mushrooms
$1/4$ to $1/2$ teaspoon red pepper flakes
1 cup shredded cabbage
$1/2$ cup defatted chicken broth
12 ounces lump crabmeat
$1/3$ cup lowfat ricotta cheese
$1/2$ cup egg substitute
$1/2$ teaspoon horseradish
$1/4$ cup freshly grated Romano cheese
salt and pepper to taste
$1 1/2$ cups White Cream Sauce No. 1 or No. 2, substituting
    champagne for white wine (page 32 or 33)

Make pasta dough of choice. Divide dough in half and shape into 2 balls. Wrap each in plastic wrap. Let one dough ball rest while preparing the filling. Refrigerate the other for another use.

Sauté red pepper, onion, mushrooms, red pepper flakes, and cabbage in broth until liquid evaporates. Stir in crabmeat, ricotta, egg substitute, horseradish, cheese, salt, and pepper. Set aside while rolling and cutting pasta dough.

Roll out dough into a 12 × 16-inch rectangle. Lay pasta on a double layer of cheesecloth or a large, thin tea towel, making sure at least 2 inches of cloth show on all sides of the pasta. Spread filling evenly on the pasta, leaving a 1-inch edge of pasta showing. Using the cloth to help, roll up pasta like a jelly roll as tightly as you can. Wrap cloth tightly around pasta and tie ends with kitchen twine.

Place roll on a rack in a roasting pan or a fish poacher. Pour in boiling water to cover and cook, covered, for 35 to 40 minutes. Remove from water and let sit 5 minutes. Cut twine and remove roll to a platter. Slice roll and serve white sauce on the side or ladle sauce onto the platter and place sliced roll on top for an elegant presentation.

Each serving provides:

452	Calories	61 g	Carbohydrate
29 g	Protein	168 mg	Cholesterol
6 g	Fat	3 g	Dietary Fiber

Linguine Niçoise

This recipe uses common Niçoise ingredients in a hot pasta instead of a salad.

Makes 6 servings

1 clove garlic, minced
1 tablespoon minced onion
$^1/_2$ cup diced sweet red pepper
2 tomatoes, peeled, seeded, and diced
1 tablespoon drained tiny capers
1 tablespoon chopped fresh basil
5 Niçoise olives, pitted and minced
2 cups White Cream Sauce No. 1 or No. 2 (page 32 or 33)
1 can (6$^1/_2$ ounces) water-packed white tuna, drained
1 hard boiled egg, chopped
1 to 1$^1/_2$ teaspoons of freshly ground black pepper
salt to taste
12 ounces linguine

Sauté garlic and onion in a pan that has been sprayed with vegetable spray until onion softens. Add red pepper, tomatoes, capers, basil, and olives. Sauté 2 minutes. Pour in sauce and warm over low heat. Blend in tuna and egg. Season with salt and pepper and warm sauce thoroughly.

Meanwhile, bring water to a boil, add pasta, and cook until al dente. Drain and toss with sauce.

Each serving provides:

378	Calories	53 g	Carbohydrate
29 g	Protein	58 mg	Cholesterol
4 g	Fat	4 g	Dietary Fiber

Seafood-Stuffed Noodles with Cognac Sauce

You can use large pasta shells or cannelloni tubes in place of the rolled lasagna noodles called for in this recipe.

Makes 6 servings

12 lasagna noodles
$1/2$ pound shrimp, shelled, deveined, and chopped
$1/2$ pound cooked crabmeat
$1/2$ pound sole, chopped
$1/3$ cup chopped green onion
2 tablespoons chopped fresh parsley
1 tablespoon fresh dill
1 teaspoon lemon zest
$1/2$ cup lowfat ricotta
2 egg whites
2 tablespoons dry unseasoned bread crumbs
salt and pepper to taste
3 tablespoons Cognac
3 cups White Cream Sauce No. 1 or No. 2, substituting
    fish broth or clam juice in place of the chicken broth
    (page 32 or 33)
$1/3$ cup freshly grated Romano cheese

Preheat oven to 350 degrees.

Cook lasagna noodles until al dente, drain, and place in cold water for 5 minutes. Drain and lay out on damp tea towels.

Put shrimp, crab, sole, green onion, 1 tablespoon of the parsley, dill, lemon zest, ricotta, egg whites, bread crumbs, salt, and pepper in a large bowl. Mix well.

Stir Cognac into white sauce. Spoon a thin layer of sauce into the bottom of a gratin dish that has been sprayed with vegetable spray.

Take a noodle and spread the fish mixture evenly on it. Roll up the noodle as tightly as you can without squeezing out the filling. Stand the roll up in the gratin dish. Repeat the process with the remaining lasagna noodles, placing them in the dish, allowing them to touch one another so that the filling does not come out. Pour remaining sauce over all. Sprinkle with cheese, cover, and bake for 20 minutes. Remove cover and bake another 10 minutes, or until hot and bubbling. Sprinkle with the remaining tablespoon of parsley.

Each serving provides:

485	Calories	58 g	Carbohydrate
43 g	Protein	139 mg	Cholesterol
6 g	Fat	2 g	Dietary Fiber

Shrimp and Scallops in Jalapeño Sauce

When cooking with fresh chile peppers, be very careful that you do not touch your eyes after working with them.

Makes 8 servings

2 tablespoons fat-free cream cheese
2 cups White Cream Sauce No. 1 or No. 2 (page 32 or 33)
6 cloves garlic, chopped
2 shallots, chopped
1/4 cup grated carrot
2 small fresh jalapeños, minced
2 teaspoons virgin olive oil
1/2 cup fish broth or clam juice
1/3 cup dry white wine
1/2 pound shrimp, peeled and deveined
3/4 pound scallops
1 1/2 tablespoons chopped cilantro
salt and pepper to taste
1 pound fusilli
freshly grated dry Jack cheese for garnish

Blend cream cheese into white sauce until melted. Set aside.

Slowly sauté garlic, shallots, carrot, and jalapeños in olive oil until garlic begins to brown. Add broth, wine, and shrimp and cook until shrimp begins to turn pink. Add scallops and cook 2 minutes more. Blend in white sauce. Warm carefully over

very low heat just until smooth and hot. Add cilantro, salt,
and pepper.

Meanwhile, bring water to a boil, add pasta, and cook until
al dente. Drain and toss with sauce. Garnish with cheese.

Each serving provides:

333	Calories	49 g	Carbohydrate
23 g	Protein	62 mg	Cholesterol
4 g	Fat	4 g	Dietary Fiber

Linguine and Calamari in Roasted Garlic-Cheese Sauce

Makes 4 servings

1 head roasted garlic (page 10)
$1/2$ cup defatted chicken broth
1 tablespoon fresh lemon balm
2 tablespoons chopped fresh basil
1 tablespoon chopped fresh parsley
2 Italian plum tomatoes, peeled, seeded, and chopped
     juice of 1 lemon
1 can (12 ounces) lite evaporated milk
$1/4$ cup freshly grated Parmesan cheese
3 tablespoons dry white wine mixed with $1 1/2$ tablespoons
     cornstarch
salt and pepper to taste
8 ounces calamari, cut into thin rings about $1/4$ inch thick
3 cups water
3 slices lemon
2 teaspoons old bay seasoning
1 bay leaf
8 ounces linguine

Squeeze roasted garlic from cloves and whisk into broth.
Cook in a saucepan for 1 minute. Mix in lemon balm, basil,
parsley, tomato, lemon juice, evaporated milk, Parmesan, and
wine mixture. Cook slowly over low heat until sauce begins
to thicken slightly. Season with salt and pepper to taste.

Cook the calamari in the water with lemon slices, old bay seasoning, and bay leaf. Cook for 1 to 2 minutes, or until tender, and drain.

Meanwhile, cook linguine until al dente, drain, and toss with calamari and sauce.

Each serving provides:

410	Calories	65 g	Carbohydrate
27 g	Protein	141 mg	Cholesterol
4 g	Fat	3 g	Dietary Fiber

Orzo and Crab Cakes with Cucumber Sauce

You can also make these cakes using salmon.

Makes 4 servings

Crab Cakes

> 1 cup cooked orzo
> 12 ounces lump crabmeat
> 2 tablespoons minced celery
> 2 tablespoons minced sweet red pepper
> 2 tablespoons minced green onion
> $1/4$ cup egg substitute
> 2 tablespoons chopped fresh dill
> salt and pepper to taste
> $1/3$ cup egg substitute
> $1/3$ cup all-purpose unbleached flour
> $2/3$ cup cracker crumbs
> 1 tablespoon dried parsley flakes

Cucumber Sauce

> $1/2$ cup peeled, seeded, and minced cucumber
> 1 teaspoon minced fresh jalapeño pepper
> 2 teaspoons fresh dill
> $1/2$ teaspoon dry mustard
> $1/2$ cup strained nonfat yogurt (page 10)
> $1/2$ teaspoon horseradish
> 1 tablespoon reduced-fat mayonnaise
> lemon pepper and salt to taste

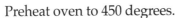

Preheat oven to 450 degrees.

Mix orzo and crab in a large bowl and set aside.

In a pan sprayed with vegetable spray, cook celery, red pepper, and green onion until vegetables are just softened. Mix vegetables with crab mixture. Add 1/4 cup egg substitute, dill, salt, and pepper and mix carefully.

Put the 1/3 cup egg substitute in one bowl, the flour in another bowl, and the cracker crumbs in a third bowl.

Form the crab mixture into 2-inch balls and flatten slightly with the palm of your hand. Dip crab cakes in egg substitute, then the flour, then egg again, and then into the cracker crumbs. Put cakes on a cookie sheet that has been sprayed with vegetable spray. Spray the top of the cakes with butter-flavored vegetable spray and bake for 5 minutes. Turn cakes over and cook 5 to 7 more minutes, or until browned.

To make sauce, blend together cucumber, jalapeño, dill, mustard, yogurt, horseradish, mayonnaise, salt, and pepper. Sauce may be warmed over low heat, if desired. Serve cakes with cucumber sauce.

Each serving provides:

368	Calories	48 g	Carbohydrate
28 g	Protein	94 mg	Cholesterol
5 g	Fat	2 g	Dietary Fiber

Spaghetti with Lobster Sauce

This is a delicious and affordable way to enjoy lobster.

Makes 6 servings

2 teaspoons butter
1 pound lobster meat, diced in 3/4-inch pieces
2 large cloves garlic, minced
1 cup quartered button mushrooms
2 tablespoons brandy
1 large tomato, peeled, seeded, and diced
1/4 cup leek, white part only, cut julienne
1 small carrot, cut julienne
1/2 cup clam juice
1 cup lite evaporated milk
salt and pepper to taste
12 ounces spaghetti
freshly grated Parmesan cheese for garnish
snipped fresh chives for garnish

Heat a nonstick pan. When hot, add butter, lobster, garlic, and mushrooms and sauté, shaking the pan, for 1 to 2 minutes. Add the brandy, ignite, and shake the pan until the flame dies down. Remove lobster mixture to a hot plate and set aside.

Put tomato, leek, carrot, and clam juice into same pan. Cook until leek and carrot soften slightly. Stir in evaporated milk and season with salt and pepper to taste. Warm, but do not let come to a boil.

Meanwhile, bring water to a boil, add pasta, and cook until al dente. Drain and place in a large serving bowl.

Return lobster mixture to sauce, blending and warming until well heated. Pour over spaghetti and garnish with Parmesan and chives.

Each serving provides:

351	Calories	50 g	Carbohydrate
27 g	Protein	61 mg	Cholesterol
4 g	Fat	3 g	Dietary Fiber

Tender Prawns and Jalapeño Pasta

This recipe takes a little advance preparation and has many ingredients, but the final result is worth all the time and effort.

Makes 4 servings

6 large fresh basil leaves, slivered
4 large fresh sage leaves, slivered
4 cloves garlic, peeled and left whole
1 small jalapeño pepper, chopped
1 teaspoon virgin olive oil
$1/2$ cup defatted chicken broth
8 ounces Jalapeño Pasta, cut into fettuccine (page 16)
12 large prawns, peeled and deveined
1 teaspoon chili sauce
2 teaspoons virgin olive oil
juice of 1 lime
juice of 1 orange
1 garlic clove, minced
$1/2$ teaspoon cumin
$1/2$ teaspoon cayenne pepper
kosher salt to taste
$1/4$ cup nonfat sour cream
1 cup evaporated milk mixed with 3 teaspoons cornstarch
1 small tomato, peeled, seeded, and diced small
salt and pepper to taste
1 tablespoon minced fresh basil for garnish

Mix basil, sage, garlic, jalapeño, 1 teaspoon olive oil, and broth in a bowl. Cover and refrigerate overnight.

Prepare pasta and let dry while preparing sauce and prawns.

Put the prawns in a glass bowl. In a measuring cup, whisk the chili sauce, 2 teaspoons olive oil, juices, minced garlic, cumin, cayenne, and salt until well blended. Pour over the prawns and marinate in refrigerator for 2 hours.

To make the sauce, strain the basil mixture that was refrigerated overnight, discarding the solids. Whisk in the sour cream and evaporated milk mixture. Put into a saucepan, add tomato and season with salt and pepper. Warm over very low heat so that the sauce does not separate.

Bring water to a boil for the pasta. Meanwhile, grill the shrimp over hot coals until they turn pink. Cook pasta, drain, and place on a platter. Lay the grilled prawns on the pasta and pour the sauce over the prawns. Sprinkle with basil.

Each serving provides:

310	Calories	39 g	Carbohydrate
25 g	Protein	170 mg	Cholesterol
6 g	Fat	1 g	Dietary Fiber

Curry Pasta with Shrimp in Yogurt Sauce

This is a delightful variant of shrimp curry.

Makes 4 servings

2 tablespoons currants
3 tablespoons brandy
8 ounces Curry Pasta, cut into fettuccine (page 16)
12 ounces shrimp, peeled and deveined
1 clove garlic, minced
3 tablespoons minced onion
$1/2$ cup defatted chicken broth or vegetable broth
8 ounces clam juice mixed with $1 1/2$ tablespoons flour
$1/2$ cup lowfat coconut milk
$1/2$ teaspoon cardamon
$1/2$ teaspoon cinnamon
$1/3$ cup nonfat sour cream
2 tablespoons chopped raw peanuts
salt and pepper to taste

Soak currants in brandy for at least 1 hour.

Make pasta and set aside.

Put shrimp, garlic, and onion in a pan with the broth and cook until shrimp turns pink and liquid evaporates. Add clam juice mixture, coconut milk, cardamon, and cinnamon and cook over medium heat, stirring to blend, until slightly thickened. Add currants with the brandy they soaked in, sour cream, and peanuts and over very low heat, stir until just blended. Season with salt and pepper.

Meanwhile, bring water to a boil, add pasta, and cook until al dente. Drain and place in a large serving bowl. Pour sauce over pasta and toss.

Each serving provides:

326	Calories	37 g	Carbohydrate
24 g	Protein	222 mg	Cholesterol
6 g	Fat	2 g	Dietary Fiber

Bow Pasta with Tuna in Fresh Pea Sauce

This is an old-time casserole dish that kids will love.

Makes 6 servings

1 pound fresh garden peas, shelled (about 2 1/2 cups)
2 cups Mushroom Sauce, substituting chicken broth for
    beef broth (page 30)
1/4 cup lemon juice
zest of 1 lemon
2 cans (6 ounces each) water-packed white tuna, drained
12 ounces bow-shaped noodles, cooked and drained
nonfat milk, if needed
salt and pepper to taste
2 tablespoons freshly grated Romano cheese

Preheat oven to 350 degrees.
    Put 1 quart water in a saucepan and bring to a boil. Add peas and blanch, about 2 to 3 minutes. Drain and place in cold water. Take 3/4 cup of the peas, drain, and purée. Set aside.
    Put mushroom sauce in a pan. Add puréed peas, lemon juice, and lemon zest. Blend well. Add whole peas and tuna and blend. Stir in pasta and add a little milk if too thick. Correct

seasoning with salt and pepper to taste. Pour into a baking dish sprayed with vegetable spray. Sprinkle with cheese. Bake, covered, for 20 to 25 minutes, or until lightly browned.

Each serving provides:

372	Calories	58 g	Carbohydrate
28 g	Protein	21 mg	Cholesterol
3 g	Fat	6 g	Dietary Fiber

Hot Pepper and Shrimp with Spaghetti

Never take deep breaths when sautéing or steaming red pepper flakes.
It can irritate your air passages.

Makes 6 servings

1 1/2 pounds shrimp, peeled and deveined
1 tablespoon virgin olive oil
1/4 cup defatted chicken broth
1/4 cup minced onion
2 cloves garlic, minced
1/2 teaspoon red pepper flakes or more to taste
5 tomatoes, peeled, seeded, and puréed
1 tablespoon chopped fresh dill
1/3 cup clam juice
1/3 cup dry white wine
salt and pepper to taste
10 ounces spaghetti
3 tablespoons freshly grated Asiago cheese

Sauté shrimp in olive oil in a nonstick pan until shrimp turns pink. Remove shrimp and set aside.

Pour broth into pan and add onion, garlic, and red pepper flakes. Cook until liquid evaporates. Add tomatoes, dill, clam juice, and wine and cook for 5 minutes over low heat. Season with salt and pepper to taste and cook 10 minutes more. Add shrimp and cook 1 minute or until mixture is hot.

Meanwhile, bring water to a boil, add pasta, and cook until al dente. Drain and put on a platter. Pour shrimp sauce over spaghetti. Garnish with freshly grated cheese.

❖

Each serving provides:

337	Calories	43 g	Carbohydrate
27 g	Protein	176 mg	Cholesterol
6 g	Fat	4 g	Dietary Fiber

Lemon Tagliatelle with Salmon in Cucumber-Tarragon Sauce

Salmon is higher in fat than white fish, so you may want to substitute sea bass or halibut. This dish makes a beautiful summer luncheon presentation: Decorate one side of the plate with thinly fanned cucumber and radish slices dotted with red caviar. Mound the tagliatelle and salmon onto the plate and drizzle with the cucumber sauce. Finish the look with curls of Parmesan cheese, made using a vegetable peeler.

Makes 4 servings

12 ounces fresh salmon fillet

1 teaspoon butter, melted

2 teaspoons Worcestershire sauce

1 tablespoon lemon juice

2 teaspoons plus 2 tablespoons chopped fresh tarragon

1 cup peeled, seeded, and diced cucumber

1 green onion, sliced thin

1/4 cup dry vermouth

1/2 cup clam juice (reserve 2 tablespoons)

1/2 cup nonfat sour cream

1/2 cup lite evaporated milk

1 tablespoon reduced-fat mayonnaise

salt and pepper to taste

11/2 tablespoons cornstarch

8 ounces lemon fettuccine

Parmesan curls for garnish

Put salmon in a dish. Whisk together butter, Worcestershire sauce, lemon juice, and 2 teaspoons of the tarragon and rub into both sides of salmon. Let salmon marinate for 15 minutes. Grill or broil the salmon about 5 minutes a side, until fish flakes. When done, cut in bite-size pieces and set aside.

Put cucumber, green onion, the remaining 2 tablespoons tarragon, and vermouth into a pan and cook 1 minute. Add clam juice, sour cream, evaporated milk, and mayonnaise. Season with salt and pepper to taste. Over very low heat, warm sauce until hot and well blended. Mix reserved 2 tablespoons of clam juice with cornstarch. Add cornstarch mixture and stir until sauce thickens.

Meanwhile, bring water to a boil, add pasta, and cook until al dente. Drain and put on a plate. Top with salmon. Drizzle with sauce and garnish with Parmesan curls.

❖

Each serving provides:

462	Calories	57 g	Carbohydrate
32 g	Protein	61 mg	Cholesterol
10 g	Fat	3 g	Dietary Fiber

Linguine and Scallops in Hot Paprika Cream Sauce

Sweet Hungarian paprika gives this dish a beautiful rosy finish. If you do not like spicy foods, omit the hot paprika.

Makes 4 servings

1 pound scallops
2 cloves garlic, minced
3 tablespoons thinly sliced green onion
1/3 cup dry white wine
2 teaspoons virgin olive oil
1 tablespoon chopped fresh basil
1 cup sliced mushrooms
1/3 cup clam juice
3/4 cup nonfat cottage cheese
1/4 cup nonfat sour cream
1/4 cup nonfat milk
1 tablespoon sweet Hungarian paprika
pinch to 1/8 teaspoon of hot Hungarian paprika or to taste
salt and pepper to taste
8 ounces linguine
1 tablespoon chopped fresh parsley for garnish

Sauté scallops, garlic, and green onion in wine and 1 teaspoon of the olive oil. Cook on high heat until liquid evaporates, stirring a few times to cook scallops through. Sprinkle with basil and remove to a plate. In same pan, add remaining teaspoon of the olive oil and mushrooms and cook for 2 minutes. Stir in clam juice and simmer 2 more minutes.

Put cottage cheese in a blender and blend until smooth. Add sour cream and blend again. Add the milk and paprikas and blend once more. Pour mixture into the pan with mushrooms. Add scallops and warm over very low heat until mixture is warmed through. Season with salt and pepper to taste.

Meanwhile, bring water to a boil, add pasta, and cook until al dente. Drain and place in a large serving bowl. Pour sauce over pasta, sprinkle with parsley, and serve.

Each serving provides:

398	Calories	53 g	Carbohydrate
34 g	Protein	40 mg	Cholesterol
5 g	Fat	3 g	Dietary Fiber

Halibut with Lemon Caper Sauce

Sorrel, with its tart lemony flavor, is a wonderful herb to use with fish. Lemon fettuccine is available in most supermarkets.

Makes 4 servings

2 tablespoons minced red onion
3 cloves garlic, minced
1/4 cup chopped fresh sorrel
2 teaspoons butter
2 tablespoons drained tiny capers
juice of 1 lemon
1 cup clam juice
salt and pepper to taste
1 cup lite evaporated milk
8 ounces Lemon Pasta, cut into fettuccine (page 16)
1 pound halibut, skin removed and cut into 1-inch dice
1 tablespoon chopped fresh parsley for garnish
1 tablespoon freshly grated Parmesan cheese

Sauté red onion, garlic, and sorrel in butter for 2 minutes. Add capers, lemon juice, clam juice, salt, and pepper and cook for 3 minutes. Stir in evaporated milk and gently warm 1 minute.

Meanwhile, bring water to a boil, cook pasta until al dente, and drain. In a pan that has been sprayed with olive oil spray, sauté the halibut until done, about 5 to 6 minutes. Set aside.

Carefully toss pasta with sauce. Add halibut and fold in gently. Serve garnished with parsley and cheese.

Each serving provides:

433	Calories	56 g	Carbohydrate
36 g	Protein	43 mg	Cholesterol
7 g	Fat	3 g	Dietary Fiber

Spaghetti with Clams in Marinara Sauce

Chili sauce can be found in the Oriental sections in most supermarkets — there are many brands to choose from. I prefer those that are spicy and very hot.

Makes 8 servings

1 small onion, minced
1 tablespoon virgin olive oil
1 cup sliced mushrooms
1 cup chopped celery
$1/4$ cup grated carrot
2 cloves garlic, minced
3 tablespoons chopped fresh parsley
$1/2$ cup defatted chicken broth
1 can (15 ounces) whole tomatoes, chopped
1 bottle (8 ounces) clam juice
$1/2$ to $3/4$ teaspoon chili sauce
12 ounces chopped canned clams
$1/4$ cup dry red wine
salt and pepper to taste
1 pound spaghetti

Sauté onion in olive oil. Add mushrooms, celery, carrot, garlic, parsley, and broth and cook 5 minutes. Add tomatoes, clam juice, chili sauce, clams, and wine. Cook for 10 minutes more. Season to taste with salt and pepper.

Meanwhile, bring water to a boil, add pasta, and cook until al dente. Drain and place in a serving bowl. Serve sauce over spaghetti.

❖

Each serving provides:

315	Calories	52 g	Carbohydrate
16 g	Protein	20 mg	Cholesterol
4 g	Fat	4 g	Dietary Fiber

9

Pasta with Poultry

Shell Pasta and Sausage Loaf with Lemon Cream Sauce

You'll love this loaf served cold at a picnic. When chilled, the flavors intensify and the sauce is unnecessary.

Makes 8 servings

1 tablespoon dry unseasoned bread crumbs

Sausage Loaf

    12 ounces small shell noodles, cooked and drained

    1 teaspoon virgin olive oil

    3 chicken breast halves, skinned

    1 parsnip, shredded

    1 cup shredded cabbage

    1 cup sliced mushrooms

    1 small onion, chopped

    3 cloves garlic, minced

    1/2 cup defatted chicken broth

    1 teaspoon *each* fennel, oregano, and basil

    2 tablespoons chopped fresh parsley

    2 tablespoons dry unseasoned bread crumbs

    3/4 cup egg substitute

    salt and pepper to taste

Lemon Cream Sauce

    1 can (12 ounces) lite evaporated milk mixed with
        3 tablespoons cornstarch

    juice of 1 large lemon

    zest of 1 lemon

2 green onions, minced
2 tablespoons minced fresh basil
2 tablespoons freshly grated Romano cheese
salt and pepper to taste

Preheat oven to 375 degrees.

Spray a ring mold or loaf pan with vegetable spray. Sprinkle with the 1 tablespoon bread crumbs. In a large bowl, toss pasta with olive oil.

Poach chicken, dice, and mix with pasta.

Sauté parsnip, cabbage, mushrooms, onion, and garlic in broth until liquid evaporates. Add sautéed vegetables to bowl with chicken and pasta. Add herbs, parsley, the 2 tablespoons bread crumbs, egg substitute, and salt and pepper to pasta mixture and mix well. Spoon into prepared pan and press down firmly. Cover with a piece of foil sprayed with vegetable spray. Bake for 40 to 50 minutes. Remove from oven and let stand for 5 minutes. Turn out onto a platter and let sit another 10 minutes.

To make sauce, mix evaporated milk mixture, lemon juice, lemon zest, green onions, basil, cheese, salt, and pepper and cook over low heat about 3 to 5 minutes, until sauce begins to thicken. Slice loaf and serve with sauce.

Each serving provides:

307	Calories	46 g	Carbohydrate
23 g	Protein	31 mg	Cholesterol
3 g	Fat	4 g	Dietary Fiber

Pappardelle with Chicken in Dijonaise Sauce

This dish looks so tantalizing, I'm sure you'll want to make it for company. If you prefer a more robust taste, add more Dijon mustard.

Makes 6 servings

4 chicken breasts, boned, skinned, and cut in 1-inch dice
2 teaspoons virgin olive oil
$1/2$ small onion, cut in wedges
1 sweet green pepper, sliced
2 yellow zucchini, sliced thinly on the diagonal
1 cup broccoli flowerets
1 tablespoon chopped fresh basil
2 teaspoons chopped fresh oregano
1 cup defatted chicken broth
2 teaspoons Dijon mustard or to taste
1 cup lite evaporated milk
3 tablespoons whiskey mixed with $1^{1}/2$ tablespoons cornstarch
salt and pepper to taste
12 ounces pappardelle

Sauté chicken in olive oil until pink is all gone. Remove chicken from pan and set aside. Into the same pan, add onion, green pepper, zucchini, broccoli, basil, oregano, and broth and cook about 5 minutes, until vegetables are tender. Add chicken and Dijon mustard and cook, stirring, until mustard is well incorporated. Remove from heat and add evaporated milk, blending well. Stir in whiskey mixture. Return to low heat and cook until slightly thickened. Season with salt and pepper.

Meanwhile, bring water to a boil, add pasta, and cook until al dente. Drain and toss with sauce.

Each serving provides:

385	Calories	52 g	Carbohydrate
30 g	Protein	51 mg	Cholesterol
5 g	Fat	6 g	Dietary Fiber

Turkey Lasagna Rolls in Red Pepper Sauce

Makes 8 servings

Turkey Lasagna Rolls

$1^{1}/_{2}$ pound turkey breast half, skin removed

1 can (28 ounces) tomato sauce

1 teaspoon dried sage leaves

1 teaspoon dried basil

1 small onion, diced

1 can (11 ounces) corn niblets, drained

2 stalks celery, minced

$^{1}/_{2}$ cup shredded carrot

2 tablespoons chopped fresh parsley

2 tablespoons slivered almonds

2 tablespoons dry unseasoned bread crumbs

$^{1}/_{4}$ cup egg substitute

salt and pepper to taste

1 pound lasagna noodles

Red Pepper Sauce

1 small onion, chopped

$1^{1}/_{2}$ cups defatted chicken broth

1 jar (12 ounces) fire-roasted red peppers, puréed

1 tablespoon fresh basil, chopped

$^{1}/_{2}$ teaspoon sugar

$^{1}/_{2}$ cup dry white wine

salt and pepper to taste

freshly grated dry Jack cheese for garnish

Preheat oven to 350 degrees.

Put turkey, tomato sauce, sage, basil, and onion in a baking dish, cover, and cook for 1 hour 20 minutes. Remove meat and shred. Place shredded turkey in a large bowl and add the sauce remaining in baking dish. Add corn and mix. Set aside.

Put celery and carrot in a pan with 1/3 cup water and cook until liquid evaporates. Add celery mixture, parsley, almonds, bread crumbs, egg substitute, salt, and pepper to turkey mixture. Mix well.

Place sauce ingredients in a blender or food processor and blend well.

Cook lasagna noodles in boiling water for 1 minute. Drain and place in cold water. Drain again and lay out on damp tea towels. Take a noodle and spread evenly with turkey filling. Roll noodle up. Put 1/2 cup of the sauce in a baking dish that has been sprayed with vegetable spray. Place lasagna roll, seam side down, in pan and continue until all noodles are done. Pour rest of sauce over noodles and cover. Cover and cook for 30 minutes. Remove cover and cook 10 minutes more or until sauce is bubbling. Sprinkle with cheese and serve.

Each serving provides:

418	Calories	61 g	Carbohydrate
33 g	Protein	53 mg	Cholesterol
5 g	Fat	5 g	Dietary Fiber

Chicken and Spaghetti in Tarragon-Artichoke Sauce

The tarragon and whiskey infuse this dish with a superb flavor.

Makes 4 servings

4 chicken breasts, boned and skinned
1 onion, peeled and cut in quarters
1 bay leaf
2 sprigs parsley
2 cups defatted chicken broth
1 package (9 ounces) frozen artichoke hearts, defrosted
2 tablespoons chopped fresh tarragon
1 tablespoon chopped fresh parsley
2 green onions, sliced
$1/2$ teaspoon Kitchen Bouquet
$1/2$ cup nonfat milk mixed with 3 teaspoons cornstarch
2 to 3 tablespoons whiskey to taste
salt and pepper to taste
8 ounces spaghetti

Put chicken, onion, bay leaf, parsley, and 6 cups of water in a large soup pot and cook over medium-high heat until chicken is done, about 15 to 20 minutes. Remove chicken and dice. Set aside.

Put broth and artichoke hearts in a saucepan and cook over medium heat for 5 minutes. Add tarragon, parsley, green onions, Kitchen Bouquet and stir well to blend. Remove pan from heat and stir in milk mixture. Return pan to low heat and cook until sauce thickens. Stir in chicken, whiskey, salt, and pepper and cook over low heat 1 minute, just to blend and warm thoroughly.

Meanwhile, bring water to a boil, add pasta, and cook until al dente. Drain and put on platter. Cover with sauce and serve.

Each serving provides:

439	Calories	59 g	Carbohydrate
40 g	Protein	69 mg	Cholesterol
3 g	Fat	4 g	Dietary Fiber

Chicken and Linguine
with Raspberry Demiglace Sauce

Use a very hot cast-iron pan to get a nice, brown crispness on meat, with little added fat. Spray with vegetable spray after the pan is very hot.

Makes 6 servings

3 whole chicken breasts, boned, skinned, and halved

$1/4$ cup seedless raspberry jam

$1/2$ cup defatted chicken broth

2 cloves garlic, minced

$1/4$ cup sliced green onions

2 tablespoons toasted pine nuts

$1/4$ cup lite evaporated milk mixed with 2 teaspoons cornstarch

2 tablespoons nonfat sour cream

2 tablespoons Chambord (optional)

salt and white pepper to taste

10 ounces linguine

1 tablespoon chopped fresh parsley for garnish

Brown chicken slightly using a very hot cast-iron pan sprayed with vegetable spray. Remove chicken and stir in jam, broth, and garlic. Boil for 1 minute to remove bits from bottom of pan. Reduce heat and add chicken. Cook for 5 to 8 minutes, or until chicken is done, but still moist.

Stir in green onion, pine nuts, and evaporated milk mixture. Over very low heat, simmer for 30 seconds to 1 minute, until sauce thickens slightly. Stir in sour cream and Chambord. Season with salt and pepper to taste.

Meanwhile, bring water to a boil, add pasta, and cook until al dente. Drain and divide among plates. Slice chicken in thin pieces. Lay a sliced chicken breast on top of linguine and spoon sauce over all. Garnish with parsley.

Each serving provides:

384	Calories	50 g	Carbohydrate
36 g	Protein	68 mg	Cholesterol
4 g	Fat	2 g	Dietary Fiber

Shells Stuffed with Chicken and Vegetables

Grilling the chicken and vegetables makes this dish outstanding.

Makes 10 servings

Stuffed Shells

> 20 jumbo pasta shells
> 1 whole chicken breast, boned and skinned
> 1 sweet green pepper, cut in half
> 1 small onion, skinned, cut in half
> 8 asparagus spears
> 1 medium zucchini, cut in half
> 3 large tomatoes
> 1/2 cup nonfat Italian dressing
> 2 medium potatoes
> 2 tablespoons nonfat milk
> salt and pepper to taste
> 1/4 cup egg substitute

Sauce

> 1/2 cup dry red wine
> 2 cups defatted chicken broth
> 1 tablespoon minced fresh oregano
> 2 tablespoons flat leaf parsley, chopped
> 1/4 cup freshly grated Asiago cheese

Preheat oven to 350 degrees.

Cook pasta shells to al dente, drain, and put in cold water. Drain again and lay out on damp tea towels.

Put chicken, green pepper, onion, asparagus, zucchini, and tomatoes in a bowl and toss with dressing. Grill chicken until done, about 12 minutes, and vegetables until they have brown grill marks on them, about 2–3 minutes. Mince the tomatoes and set aside for the sauce. Put the green pepper in a plastic bag and seal. Let rest for 10 minutes. Remove pepper and, with a sharp knife, remove most of the skin (leave on some charred bits of skin). Mince chicken and vegetables and put into a bowl.

Cook potatoes until tender and mash with milk. Season with salt and pepper. Mix in with vegetables and chicken. Stir in egg substitute. Fill shells with chicken and vegetable mixture and set aside.

To make sauce, cook grilled tomatoes, wine, broth, oregano, and parsley over medium heat for 10 minutes. Put a thin layer of sauce in bottom of a 10-inch round baking pan that has been sprayed with vegetable spray. Put stuffed shells in a single layer in pan and cover with remaining sauce. Sprinkle with cheese. Cover with foil and bake for 25 minutes. Remove cover and cook 10 minutes more.

Each serving provides:

198	Calories	32 g	Carbohydrate
12 g	Protein	18 mg	Cholesterol
2 g	Fat	3 g	Dietary Fiber

Chicken and Artichokes on Penne

This dish is so flavorful, it's hard to believe there is so little fat.

Makes 8 servings

8 chicken breast halves, boned and skinned
1 medium onion, sliced thin
2 garlic cloves, minced
5 tomatoes, peeled, seeded, and puréed
1/2 cup dry red wine
1 cup defatted chicken broth
1/4 cup chopped fresh parsley
2 teaspoons dried oregano
1 1/2 tablespoons red wine vinegar
1/3 cup sliced black olives
1 package (9 ounces) frozen artichoke hearts, defrosted
salt and pepper to taste
1 pound penne
2 tablespoons cornstarch mixed with 1/4 cup water
freshly grated Parmesan cheese for garnish

Heat a nonstick skillet and when very hot, spray with olive oil
spray. Cook chicken breasts a few at a time until browned on
both sides.

Remove from pan.

Spray pan again and add onion and garlic, cooking until
onion begins to soften. Add tomatoes, wine, broth, parsley,
oregano, and vinegar and blend well. Return chicken to pan
and add olives and artichokes. Cover pan and cook over

medium heat for 20 to 25 minutes. Season to taste with salt and pepper.

Meanwhile, bring water to a boil and cook pasta until al dente. Drain and turn onto a platter. Remove chicken and artichokes from pan and lay on top of the pasta. Stir cornstarch mixture into pan and cook sauce over low heat until thickened. Pour sauce over chicken and pasta. Garnish with cheese.

Each serving provides:

393	Calories	51 g	Carbohydrate
37 g	Protein	69 mg	Cholesterol
4 g	Fat	6 g	Dietary Fiber

Chicken and Pinwheel Pasta

When using fresh orange or lemon zest, make sure you wash the fruit in warm water first.

Makes 6 servings

2 whole chicken breasts
1 tablespoon honey
1 1/2 cups orange juice
6 cloves garlic, peeled and left whole
12 ounces pinwheel pasta
1 small onion, chopped
2 ounces shiitake mushrooms, sliced
1/2 cup dry white wine
1/2 cup defatted chicken broth
2 tablespoons soy sauce mixed with 2 tablespoons cornstarch
1 teaspoon grated fresh ginger
2 teaspoons *each* minced cilantro and orange zest for garnish

Preheat oven to 375 degrees.

Put chicken, skin side up, in a roasting pan sprayed with vegetable spray. Mix the honey with 1/2 cup of the orange juice. Pour over chicken and sprinkle garlic cloves around chicken. Bake for 20 minutes. Remove chicken. Peel off skin and discard. Dice chicken and set aside.

Boil water for pasta. While pasta cooks, make the sauce.

In a saucepan, put onion, mushrooms, and 1/4 cup of the orange juice and cook until liquid evaporates. Add remaining 3/4 cup of the orange juice, wine, broth, soy sauce mixture, and

ginger. Cook over low heat, stirring, until mixture thickens.
Add chicken to pan.

When pasta is done, drain, and mix with chicken and sauce.
Serve garnished with a little cilantro and orange zest.

Each serving provides:

251	Calories	51 g	Carbohydrate
8 g	Protein	0 mg	Cholesterol
1 g	Fat	4 g	Dietary Fiber

Cannelloni with Chicken and Broccoli

Use a brand of nonfat cheese that will melt and has a good texture. You may have to give several brands a try before finding one that works.

Makes 4 servings

1 whole chicken breast, boned, skinned, and ground or minced
3 shallots, minced
1 cup chopped broccoli flowerets or peeled stems
$1/2$ cup defatted chicken broth
$1/4$ cup lowfat cottage cheese
1 teaspoon dried oregano
2 egg whites
$1/2$ teaspoon salt
pepper to taste
8 cannelloni shells
3 cups White Cream Sauce No. 1 or No. 2 (page 32 or 33)
2 ounces chèvre
$1/4$ cup good-quality brandy
8 ounces grated nonfat mozzarella cheese
1 tablespoon freshly grated Romano cheese

Preheat oven to 375 degrees.

Sauté chicken in a nonstick pan that has been sprayed with olive oil spray. Cook the chicken over medium heat until done. Add shallots, broccoli, and broth. Cook until liquid evaporates.

Remove chicken and vegetables to a bowl. Add cottage cheese, oregano, egg whites, salt, and pepper and blend well. Set aside.

Cook pasta until al dente, then immediately plunge into cold water. Drain and place in a strainer until ready to stuff.

Stir chèvre into white sauce until well blended and smooth. Stir in brandy. Set aside. Spray a 10-inch round baking dish with olive oil spray and pour 1/2 cup of the sauce in the bottom of the dish. Stuff each cannelloni shell with 1/3 cup of the filling. Lay cannelloni in dish and cover with the rest of the sauce. Sprinkle with mozzarella and Romano cheese. Bake, covered, for 20 to 30 minutes. Uncover and bake for 5 to 10 minutes more, until lightly browned.

Each serving provides:

591	Calories	67 g	Carbohydrate
56 g	Protein	59 mg	Cholesterol
7 g	Fat	6 g	Dietary Fiber

Pasta with Peppers and Chicken

Not only beautiful, this dish is light, luscious, and easy.

Makes 4 servings

3 chicken breasts, boned, skinned, and cut into thin slices
2 cups defatted chicken broth
1/3 cup slivered green onion
1 sweet red pepper, slivered
1 tablespoon chopped fresh oregano
1 tablespoon chopped fresh parsley
1/2 to 3/4 teaspoon chili sauce or to taste
1/3 cup dry white wine
1/3 cup lite evaporated milk
salt and pepper to taste
8 ounces fusilli
3 teaspoons cornstarch mixed with 2 tablespoons water
    (optional)

Sauté chicken, a few slices at a time, in a very hot nonstick pan
that has been sprayed with vegetable spray. When chicken begins to brown, pour in a couple tablespoons of the broth and
cook until liquid evaporates. Remove chicken and repeat
process until all chicken is done.

Respray pan with vegetable spray and put in green onions
and cook 1 minute. Add red pepper and a couple more tablespoons of the broth. Cook until liquid evaporates. Return
chicken to pan and add remaining broth, oregano, parsley,
chili sauce, and wine. Cook for 2 minutes over low heat, add
evaporated milk (remember *not to boil* once milk is added) and

season with salt and pepper to taste. If necessary, remove from heat, stir in cornstarch mixture and return to very low heat until thickened.

Meanwhile, bring water to a boil, add pasta, and cook until al dente. Drain and toss with sauce.

Each serving provides:

340	Calories	46 g	Carbohydrate
30 g	Protein	52 mg	Cholesterol
2 g	Fat	4 g	Dietary Fiber

Corkscrew Pasta with Turkey in Dried Tomato-Basil Sauce

The turkey breast used in this recipe is half of a whole turkey breast. You could also use sliced turkey cutlets.

Makes 4 servings

1 pound turkey breast, skinned and diced
2 teaspoons virgin olive oil
$1/2$ cup plus 4 tablespoons defatted chicken broth
$1/4$ cup dried tomato, soaked for 5 minutes in 1 cup warm water
2 tablespoons slivered fresh basil
$1/3$ cup Madeira wine
$1/2$ cup slivered spinach
2 green onions, sliced thin
$1/2$ cup lite evaporated milk
salt and pepper to taste
3 teaspoons cornstarch
6 ounces corkscrew pasta
freshly grated Asiago cheese for garnish

Sauté half the turkey in 1 teaspoon of the olive oil and 1 tablespoon of the broth until done. Remove to a bowl and continue with other half turkey, remaining 1 teaspoon olive oil and another tablespoon of the broth and cook until done. Remove to same bowl.

Squeeze tomatoes and discard water. Slice into thin slivers and put in a saucepan with basil, $1/2$ cup of the broth, wine, spinach, green onions, and turkey. Cook for 3 minutes, or until spinach is done. Remove from heat and add evaporated milk and salt and pepper to taste. Warm over low heat. Mix cornstarch with the remaining 2 tablespoons of the broth. Stir into sauce until it begins to thicken.

Meanwhile, bring water to a boil, add pasta, and cook until al dente. Drain and toss with sauce. Serve with a sprinkling of grated cheese.

Each serving provides:

417	Calories	42 g	Carbohydrate
39 g	Protein	79 mg	Cholesterol
8 g	Fat	4 g	Dietary Fiber

Spaghetti and Chicken in Roasted Garlic Sauce

You can roast a whole head of garlic or just the 4 cloves needed for this recipe. I like to roast a whole head so that I have some left over to spread on bread or add to a sauce or soup.

Makes 4 servings

4 cloves roasted garlic (page 10)
3 chicken breast halves, boned, skinned, and diced
2 tablespoons thinly sliced green onion
1 cup thinly sliced mushrooms
$1/4$ to $1/2$ teaspoon red pepper flakes or to taste
$2 1/2$ cups defatted chicken broth
1 tablespoon minced fresh sage
$1/2$ cup lite evaporated milk mixed with 1 tablespoon cornstarch
3 tablespoons nonfat sour cream
salt and pepper to taste
8 ounces spaghetti, cooked and drained

Squeeze roasted garlic from cloves and set aside.

In a nonstick pan that has been sprayed with olive oil spray, sauté chicken over medium-high heat for 5 minutes, or until done. Remove chicken to a plate. Sauté green onion, mushrooms, and red pepper flakes in $1/2$ cup of the broth until liquid evaporates. Add sage, remaining 2 cups broth, and roasted garlic and cook over low heat for 5 minutes. Add chicken and cook 5 minutes more. Remove from heat and stir in cornstarch mixture, sour cream, and salt and pepper to taste. Return pan

to heat and cook over very low heat until sauce begins to
thicken.

Meanwhile, bring water to a boil, add pasta, and cook until
al dente. Drain and pour chicken and sauce over spaghetti
and serve.

Each serving provides:

379	Calories	55 g	Carbohydrate
33 g	Protein	52 mg	Cholesterol
2 g	Fat	3 g	Dietary Fiber

Tagliatelle and Chicken with Sage Cream Sauce

This subtle sauce is wonderful when served with any chicken or cornish hen dish.

Makes 4 servings

3 chicken breasts
$1/4$ cup minced onion
2 teaspoons walnut oil
2 tablespoons minced fresh sage
1 cup vegetable broth
2 tablespoons whiskey
$1/2$ cup lite evaporated milk
$1/2$ cup nonfat sour cream
1 tablespoon freshly grated Parmesan cheese
salt and pepper to taste
3 teaspoons cornstarch mixed with 2 tablespoons water
8 ounces tagliatelle or fettuccine noodles

Grill or roast chicken breasts and slice thinly. Set aside. Sauté onion in walnut oil for 1 minute. Add sage and broth and cook 3 minutes more. Add whiskey and cook 1 minute more. Turn heat off and blend in evaporated milk, sour cream, and Parmesan. Return to heat and warm on low heat until hot. Season with salt and pepper to taste. Add cornstarch mixture and stir until sauce thickens. Add chicken.

Meanwhile, bring water to a boil, add pasta, and cook until al dente. Drain and toss with sauce and chicken.

Each serving provides:

468	Calories	56 g	Carbohydrate
35 g	Protein	65 mg	Cholesterol
10 g	Fat	3 g	Dietary Fiber

Blackened Chicken Strips on Pasta with Cajun Sauce

Cajun cooking is a favorite for those of us who like hot and spicy foods.

Makes 4 servings

1/4 cup paprika

1 teaspoon garlic powder

1 teaspoon onion powder

1/8 teaspoon pepper

1 teaspoon dried fines herbes

2 whole chicken breasts, halved, skinned, and boned

1 clove garlic, minced

2 tablespoons minced onion

1 1/2 cups defatted chicken broth

1 tomato, peeled, seeded, and minced

1/4 cup dry white wine

1 tablespoon chopped fresh herbs (choose from oregano, basil, tarragon, or marjoram)

salt to taste

8 ounces penne

To make Cajun spice, mix paprika, garlic powder, onion powder, pepper, and fines herbes. Set aside.

Put chicken breasts between two pieces of wax paper and pound to flatten. Moisten breasts with water and rub with Cajun spice (reserve 1/4 teaspoon of the spice for the sauce). Spray a very hot cast-iron pan with vegetable spray and then quickly fry breasts for 4 to 6 minutes, or until done. Remove breasts and slice into thin strips. Set aside.

Sauté garlic and onion in a small pan that has been sprayed with vegetable spray, until onion is soft. Add broth, tomato, wine, fresh herbs and 1/4 teaspoon of the Cajun spice. Simmer for 8 minutes. Season with salt to taste.

Meanwhile cook pasta, drain, and place on a platter. Lay chicken on pasta and then drizzle with sauce.

Each serving provides:

383	Calories	47 g	Carbohydrate
36 g	Protein	73 mg	Cholesterol
5 g	Fat	6 g	Dietary Fiber

Fettuccine with Grilled Chicken and Vegetables

A grill basket or grill wok work wonderfully when grilling smaller vegetables. If you don't have a grill wok, cut vegetables in half and then cut smaller after grilling.

Makes 4 serving

4 chicken breast halves, boned and skinned
1 cup nonfat Italian dressing
1 medium zucchini, sliced in 1/4-inch rounds
1 carrot, sliced on the diagonal
3 pattypan squash, cut into sixths
1/2 small red onion, cut into thin wedges
1 teaspoon minced fresh basil
1 teaspoon minced fresh oregano
6 ounces fettuccine
freshly ground pepper and salt to taste
2 tablespoons freshly grated Parmesan cheese for garnish

Put chicken in a bowl and marinate in 1/2 cup of the dressing for 20 minutes. Cut vegetables and toss with basil, oregano, and remaining 1/2 cup of the dressing. Marinate until chicken is cooked.

Grill chicken, basting with marinade, for 10 to 15 minutes, or until done. Discard any leftover marinade and thinly slice the chicken. Set aside. Remove vegetables from marinade and reserve marinade. Grill vegetables until they soften and have grill marks.

Meanwhile, bring water to a boil, add pasta, and cook until al dente. Drain and place in a large serving bowl. Toss chicken, vegetables, and reserved marinade from the vegetables with hot pasta. Season with salt and pepper to taste. Sprinkle with cheese.

Each serving provides:

362	Calories	43 g	Carbohydrate
35 g	Protein	75 mg	Cholesterol
5 g	Fat	4 g	Dietary Fiber

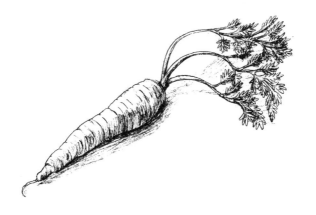

10

Pasta with Beans

Cannellini Beans and Halibut in Black Peppercorn Sauce

Makes 4 servings

12 ounces halibut
1 cup cooked cannellini beans
3 tablespoons minced sweet red pepper
1/4 cup chopped inner celery stalks with leaves included
2 green onions, sliced
1 tablespoon chopped fresh basil
8 ounces lasagnette
1 cup lite evaporated milk mixed with 2 teaspoons cornstarch
1/3 cup clam juice
1 tablespoon bourbon
1 teaspoon black peppercorns, crushed coarsely
salt to taste
Freshly grated Romano cheese for garnish

Spray a grill with vegetable spray and cook halibut over very
hot coals about 5 minutes a side, or until fish flakes. Remove
from grill. Shred fish in large pieces and place into a bowl. Toss
with beans.

In a nonstick pan, sauté red pepper, celery, green onions, and
basil with 2 tablespoons water until liquid evaporates. Add
vegetables to fish mixture.

Bring water to a boil and cook lasagnette noodles until al
dente. Drain. While noodles are cooking, put evaporated milk
mixture and clam juice in a saucepan and cook over low heat

just until mixture thickens. Stir in bourbon, peppercorns, and salt and blend. Stir in fish mixture.

Turn noodles onto a platter. Spoon sauce over noodles and garnish with cheese.

Each serving provides:

419	Calories	62 g	Carbohydrate
33 g	Protein	28 mg	Cholesterol
4 g	Fat	4 g	Dietary Fiber

Pasta, Bean, and Bok Choy Bake

This tasty baked dish can be served in a pool of Light Tomato-Basil Sauce (page 28) for a colorful presentation.

Makes 6 servings

2 tablespoons dry unseasoned bread crumbs
1/4 pound spaghetti, cooked al dente and rinsed in cold water
1 can (15 ounces) white beans, rinsed and drained
1 cup chopped bok choy, blanched and drained
1 large clove garlic, minced
1/4 cup chopped onion
1 cup sliced mushrooms
1/4 teaspoon red pepper flakes or to taste
1/4 cup vegetable broth
1 cup tomato sauce
3 tablespoons dry vermouth
1/4 cup egg substitute or 1 egg, beaten slightly
2 teaspoons dried basil
1 tablespoon chopped fresh parsley
salt and pepper to taste

Preheat oven to 350 degrees.

Spray a loaf pan or ring mold with vegetable spray and then sprinkle the bread crumbs on bottom and sides of pan. Set aside.

Mix spaghetti, white beans, and bok choy in a large bowl. Set aside.

Sauté garlic, onion, mushrooms, and red pepper flakes in broth until liquid evaporates. Stir into spaghetti mixture. Add tomato sauce, vermouth, egg, basil, parsley, salt, and pepper. Blend well.

Put into prepared pan and press to pack into pan. Cover with a piece of wax paper that has been sprayed with vegetable spray. Bake for 30 to 35 minutes. Remove from oven and discard wax paper. Let sit 10 minutes, invert, and serve.

Each serving provides:

186	Calories	36 g	Carbohydrate
8 g	Protein	0 mg	Cholesterol
1 g	Fat	5 g	Dietary Fiber

Black Bean and Orange Roughy with Roasted Pepper Fettuccine

This dish is delicious just thrown together, but when you take the time to artfully arrange the elements on each plate, it is gorgeous.

Makes 6 servings

10 ounces Fire-Roasted Red Pepper Pasta, cut into fettuccine
  (page 16)
2 cloves garlic, minced
2 green onions, cut julienne
1 small sweet yellow pepper, cut julienne
1 small carrot, cut julienne
12 ounces orange roughy, cut in $2 \times 1/2$-inch slices
$1/4$ cup plum wine mixed with 2 tablespoons water
$1/4$ cup bamboo shoots, cut julienne
1 can (15 ounces) black beans, rinsed and drained
3 tablespoons fish sauce
1 tablespoon oyster sauce
2 to 3 teaspoons lite soy sauce
1 cup water mixed with 2 teaspoons cornstarch
1 large bunch Swiss chard, cut chiffonade

Make pasta and set aside while preparing the fish and bean sauce.

Put garlic, green onions, yellow pepper, carrot, and orange roughy in wine mixture and cook over medium heat for 2 to 3 minutes, or until fish is done. Add bamboo shoots, beans, fish sauce, oyster sauce, and soy sauce and blend well. Stir in cornstarch mixture and cook, stirring, over low heat until mixture thickens.

Bring water to a boil, cook pasta until al dente, and drain. Meanwhile, cook chard in boiling water about 3 to 5 minutes, or until it turns bright green. Drain.

Divide pasta among plates, making a small circle of pasta in the center of each plate. Place chard in a ring around the pasta and mound the bean and fish mixture onto the pasta.

❖

Each serving provides:

274	Calories	37 g	Carbohydrate
17 g	Protein	43 mg	Cholesterol
6 g	Fat	4 g	Dietary Fiber

Cornmeal Pasta with Beans
in a Baked Vegetable Sauce

Cornmeal pasta is great fun to experiment with. Try making enchi-
ladas (using shredded pork or chicken), or use it in a mixed bean and
cornmeal pasta salad, or make a chicken ravioli laced with a cilantro
cream sauce — let your imagination flow.

Makes 8 servings

1 pound Cornmeal Pasta, cut into pappardelle (page 15)
5 Italian plum tomatoes, peeled and left whole
1 sweet green pepper, diced large
2 jalapeño peppers, minced
1 small parsnip, peeled and sliced in 1/2-inch rounds
1 medium onion, peeled and quartered
5 cloves garlic, peeled and left whole
2 stalks celery with leaves
2 cups defatted chicken broth
1/2 cup dry red wine
1 can (15 ounces) black beans, rinsed and drained
salt and pepper to taste
1/4 cup chopped cilantro
3 tablespoons freshly grated dry Jack cheese for garnish

Make pasta and set aside.

Preheat oven to 425 degrees.

Put tomatoes, green pepper, jalapeños, parsnip, onion, garlic,
and celery in a roasting pan that has been sprayed with vegetable spray and cook, covered, for 20 minutes. Uncover and
cook for 20 minutes more. Remove vegetables and purée in a

food processor or blender. Put purée into a saucepan with broth, wine, beans, salt, and pepper and cook for 10 minutes more. Stir in half of the cilantro.

Meanwhile, bring water to a boil, add pasta, and cook until al dente. Drain and toss with the sauce and put on a platter. Sprinkle with the other half of the cilantro and the cheese.

Each serving provides:

257	Calories	44 g	Carbohydrate
11 g	Protein	96 mg	Cholesterol
4 g	Fat	5 g	Dietary Fiber

Shrimp with Beans and Rosemary on a Bed of Linguine

If you want to cut the small amount of added fat in this recipe, omit the olive oil and cook the shrimp in a small amount of broth.

Makes 6 servings

1 pound large shrimp, peeled and deveined

2 large cloves garlic, minced

2 teaspoons virgin olive oil

$1/2$ cup defatted chicken broth

$1/2$ cup clam juice

2 large tomatoes, peeled, seeded, and chopped

1 tablespoon minced fresh rosemary

1 cup cooked cannellini or navy beans

12 ounces linguine

$1/4$ cup dry vermouth mixed with 1 tablespoon cornstarch

salt and pepper to taste

1 tablespoon chopped flat parsley for garnish

1 tablespoon freshly grated Asiago cheese for garnish

In a very hot pan, sauté shrimp and garlic in olive oil until shrimp turns pink. Remove shrimp and add broth, clam juice, tomatoes, rosemary, and beans to pan and cook 5 minutes.

Meanwhile, bring water to a boil, add pasta, and cook until al dente. Drain and place on a platter.

While pasta is cooking, return shrimp to pan with tomato mixture and remove from heat. Add cornstarch mixture. Blend

well, return to low heat, and cook, stirring, until thickened.
Season with salt and pepper to taste.

Pour sauce over pasta. Garnish with parsley and grated
cheese.

Each serving provides:

345	Calories	51 g	Carbohydrate
23 g	Protein	117 mg	Cholesterol
4 g	Fat	4 g	Dietary Fiber

Rigatoni with Cranberry Beans in Vodka Sauce

I keep a bottle of flavored vodka on hand: Add 2 tablespoons pink peppercorns to a bottle of vodka. Keep peppercorns in the bottle until vodka is gone. Since my vodka is flavored, I omit the red pepper flakes in this recipe.

Makes 4 servings

1/4 to 1/2 teaspoon red pepper flakes or to taste
2 tablespoons minced onion
2 teaspoons butter (optional)
3/4 cup defatted chicken broth
3 cups peeled and diced Italian plum tomatoes
1/2 cup chopped fresh basil
2/3 cup cooked cranberry beans
1/2 cup lite evaporated milk
1/3 cup vodka
salt and pepper to taste
8 ounces rigatoni
Asiago cheese curls for garnish

Put pepper flakes, onion, optional butter, and 1/4 cup of the broth into a saucepan and cook until liquid evaporates. Add the remaining 1/2 cup broth, the tomatoes, 1/4 cup of the basil, and beans to pan and cook until tomatoes are soft and well cooked. Remove pan from heat and add the remaining 1/4 cup of the basil, evaporated milk, vodka, and salt and pepper to taste. Return to heat on low and cook until heated through.

Meanwhile, bring water to a boil, add pasta, and cook until al dente. Drain and toss with beans and sauce. Serve with cheese.

Each serving provides:

377	Calories	68 g	Carbohydrate
16 g	Protein	1 mg	Cholesterol
2 g	Fat	9 g	Dietary Fiber

Smoky Black Beans and Zucchini with Cornmeal Pasta

Makes 4 servings

8 ounces Cornmeal Pasta, cut into fettuccine (page 15)

1/4 cup diced red onion

2 cloves garlic, minced

4 ounces Canadian bacon, diced

1/2 cup diced green zucchini

1/2 cup diced yellow zucchini

2 teaspoons butter or 1/4 cup defatted chicken broth

1 cup cooked black beans

1 recipe Light Tomato-Basil Sauce, substituting cilantro for basil
     (page 28)

salt and pepper to taste

2 tablespoons freshly grated dry Jack cheese for garnish

Make pasta and set aside.

In a nonstick pan, sauté red onion, garlic, bacon, and zucchini in butter until vegetables are just tender. Stir in black beans and tomato sauce and cook for 3 minutes to blend flavors. Correct seasoning with salt and pepper to taste.

Cook and drain cornmeal pasta. Toss with bean mixture and serve garnished with grated cheese.

Each serving provides:

357	Calories	48 g	Carbohydrate
20 g	Protein	119 mg	Cholesterol
9 g	Fat	5 g	Dietary Fiber

White Bean
and Vegetable Spaghetti

If you like your vegetables well done, add 1/2 cup more broth when cooking them, and cook 5 minutes longer.

Makes 8 servings

1 cup chopped onion
1 cup chopped carrot
1 cup sliced zucchini
1 cup sliced Japanese eggplant
1 cup cooked white beans
2 tablespoons minced fresh oregano
1 tablespoon minced fresh marjoram
2 tablespoons chopped fresh parsley
2 cups defatted chicken broth
1/3 cup dry white wine
1/4 to 1/2 teaspoon chili sauce
1/2 cup lite evaporated milk
1/2 cup nonfat sour cream
salt and white pepper to taste
12 ounces spaghetti
freshly grated Parmesan cheese for garnish

Put onion, carrot, zucchini, eggplant, beans, oregano, marjoram, parsley, and 1 cup of the broth in a saucepan and cook for 5 minutes, or until vegetables soften. Add the remaining 1 cup broth, wine, and chili sauce and cook 2 minutes more. Remove from heat and stir in milk, sour cream, and salt and pepper to taste. Return to heat and carefully warm to blend.

Meanwhile, bring water to a boil, add pasta, and cook until al dente. Pour sauce over pasta and garnish with Parmesan.

Each serving provides:

236	Calories	44 g	Carbohydrate
11 g	Protein	2 mg	Cholesterol
2 g	Fat	4 g	Dietary Fiber

MEXICAN PASTA PRIMAVERA

Shrimp, chicken, zucchini, or baby corn are all terrific additions to this pasta dish.

Makes 6 servings

1 large whole tomato, peeled and diced small
2 cloves garlic, minced
1/4 cup chopped green onion
2 tablespoons chopped cilantro
1 tablespoon diced jalapeño pepper
1 tablespoon lime juice
salt and pepper to taste
1 1/2 cups defatted chicken broth
1/2 sweet green pepper, seeded and cut into thin strips
1/2 sweet yellow pepper, seeded and cut into thin strips
3/4 cup cooked black beans
1/2 cup nonfat cottage cheese
1/2 cup nonfat sour cream
2 tablespoons nonfat milk
1 tablespoon cornstarch mixed with 3 tablespoons water
    or broth
10 ounces penne
1 tablespoon *each* chopped fresh parsley and cilantro, mixed for
    garnish
freshly grated dry Jack cheese for garnish

Put tomato, garlic, green onion, cilantro, jalapeño, lime juice, and salt and pepper in a bowl and toss to mix. Set aside.

Put broth in a pan and add sweet peppers and beans. Cook over medium heat for 2 minutes. Add tomato mixture, blending well, and cook for 1 minute more. Remove from heat.

Put the cottage cheese, sour cream, and milk in a blender, blending until smooth. Add to tomato mixture and combine well. Taste and season with additional salt and freshly ground pepper. Return to stove and warm over low heat, making sure mixture does not boil. Add cornstarch mixture and stir until thickened.

Meanwhile, bring water to a boil, add pasta, and cook until al dente. Pour sauce over pasta and toss. Serve garnished with herbs and cheese.

❖

Each serving provides:

240	Calories	46 g	Carbohydrate
13 g	Protein	1 mg	Cholesterol
1 g	Fat	5 g	Dietary Fiber

11

Homemade Gnocchi, Ravioli, and Tortellini

Cornmeal Gnocchi with Jalapeño Cream Sauce

Try this sauce on slices of roasted chicken, it is spectacular.

Makes 6 servings

Cornmeal Gnocchi

    1 cup mashed potato
    $1/2$ cup cornmeal
    $1/2$ cup all-purpose unbleached flour
    1 egg plus 1 egg white
    1 tablespoon dried cilantro
    $1/2$ teaspoon cayenne pepper
    $1/2$ teaspoon salt

Jalapeño Cream Sauce

    2 fresh jalapeño peppers, seeded and minced
    2 green onions, sliced
    2 cups White Cream Sauce No. 1 or No. 2 (page 32 or 33)
    1 tomato, peeled, seeded, and chopped
    salt and pepper to taste

To make gnocchi, mix potato, cornmeal, flour, eggs, cilantro, cayenne, and salt in a large bowl until well blended. Turn onto a floured work surface and knead for 5 minutes. Divide dough into 6 pieces. Roll each piece into cylinders $1/2$ to $3/4$ inch thick. Cut into $1/2$-inch slices. Drop into boiling water and cook until gnocchi rise to the top. Drain and place in a warmed bowl.

To make sauce, sauté jalapeños and green onion in a pan sprayed with vegetable spray until vegetables are soft. Stir in the white sauce and tomato. Season with salt and pepper to taste. Warm on low heat, until heated through. Cover gnocchi with sauce and serve.

Each serving provides:

196	Calories	34 g	Carbohydrate
9 g	Protein	39 mg	Cholesterol
2 g	Fat	2 g	Dietary Fiber

Potato and Roasted Garlic Gnocchi

Carefully add flour to gnocchi dough until the right consistency is reached. Gnocchi is like bread, pasta, and pastry in that watching and feeling the consistency of the dough is essential in getting the right texture in the final product. Don't give up with only one try.

Makes 4 servings

1 whole head garlic, roasted (page 10)
1 cup mashed potato
$1/2$ teaspoon *each* salt and pepper
1 teaspoon dried thyme leaves
1 egg white plus 1 egg, beaten
1 cup unbleached all-purpose flour
2 cups Mushroom Sauce (page 30)
Freshly grated Asiago cheese for garnish

Squeeze roasted garlic from cloves and mix with potatoes. Stir in salt, pepper, thyme, eggs, and flour. Keep mixing, adding more flour if necessary to achieve a workable dough. Knead the dough for 3 to 4 minutes on a floured surface. If dough is too sticky to handle, add a tablespoon of flour. The dough should be very soft or the gnocchi will be very heavy.

Divide dough into 6 pieces. Roll each piece into cylinders $1/2$ to $3/4$ inch thick. Cut the cylinders into $3/4$-inch slices. Drop gnocchi in boiling water and cook until gnocchi rise to the top. Drain and put on a platter. Cover with sauce and a sprinkling of cheese.

Each serving provides:

264	Calories	46 g	Carbohydrate
11 g	Protein	58 mg	Cholesterol
3 g	Fat	3 g	Dietary Fiber

Butternut Squash Ravioli in Cinnamon Orange Sauce

This makes a beautiful first course for Thanksgiving dinner.

Makes 6 servings

1 pound fresh butternut squash, cut in half and seeds removed

2 teaspoons melted butter

3 teaspoons brown sugar

salt and pepper to taste

1 recipe Orange Pasta (page 16)

3 shallots, minced

1/2 cup defatted chicken broth

1/2 cup frozen orange juice concentrate

1 tablespoon orange zest

1 teaspoon cinnamon

1/3 cup strained nonfat yogurt (page 10)

2 tablespoons Grand Marnier mixed with 1 tablespoon
　　cornstarch

1 tablespoon chopped toasted pecans

Preheat oven to 350 degrees.

　　Brush squash with melted butter and sprinkle with brown sugar and salt and pepper to taste. Put squash on a rimmed cookie sheet and cook until tender, about 40 to 45 minutes. Scoop out cooked squash and purée.

　　Make pasta and stuff ravioli with the squash purée according to the instructions on page 5.

To make the sauce, put shallots and broth in a saucepan and let cook until liquid is reduced to $1/4$ cup. Let cool. Add juice concentrate, zest, cinnamon, and yogurt, cooking over low heat until well blended. Remove from heat and add cornstarch mixture. Blend well and return to low heat and cook for about 30 seconds, or until mixture thickens.

Cook ravioli in boiling water for 3 to 5 minutes, or until ravioli rise to the top. Drain and turn onto a warm platter. Pour warm sauce over the ravioli and sprinkle with toasted pecans.

Each serving provides:

402	Calories	71 g	Carbohydrate
13 g	Protein	147 mg	Cholesterol
7 g	Fat	4 g	Dietary Fiber

Dried Tomato Tortellini in Light Cucumber Sauce

Making homemade tortellini is time consuming, but the results are very satisfying.

Makes 6 servings

Tortellini

> 4 ounces chèvre
>
> 1 package (9 ounces) artichoke hearts, defrosted and chopped
>
> 2 tablespoons chopped fresh cilantro
>
> 1/2 cup small curd lowfat cottage cheese
>
> 1/4 cup egg substitute
>
> salt and pepper to taste
>
> Dried Tomato Pasta (page 16)

Cucumber Sauce

> 1 cucumber peeled, seeded, and minced
>
> 1 tablespoon sliced green onion
>
> 1/2 cup chopped tomatillos
>
> 2 teaspoons lime juice
>
> 1/2 teaspoon dried oregano
>
> 1 1/2 cups defatted chicken broth
>
> 2 tablespoons dry white wine mixed with 1 tablespoon cornstarch
>
> salt and pepper to taste

2 tablespoons freshly grated dry Jack cheese for garnish

To make the tortellini filling, combine chèvre, artichokes, 1 tablespoon of the cilantro, cottage cheese, egg substitute, salt, and pepper and blend well.

Make pasta and fill following instructions on page 6.

To make the sauce, put cucumber, green onion, tomatillos, lime juice, oregano, and broth in a pan and slowly cook for 5 minutes. Add cornstarch mixture, stirring, over low heat and warm through until slightly thickened. Season with salt and pepper.

Cook tortellini in boiling water for 3 to 5 minutes, or until tortellini rise to the top. Drain and remove to a serving bowl. Cover with sauce and garnish with grated cheese.

Each serving provides:

409	Calories	57 g	Carbohydrate
21 g	Protein	189 mg	Cholesterol
10 g	Fat	3 g	Dietary Fiber

Chicken Ravioli
in Tarragon Cream Sauce

If you don't have the time to make fresh pasta, use wonton wrappers.

Makes 6 servings

Chicken Ravioli

> 3 chicken breasts, boned, skinned, and ground
> 1 teaspoon butter
> 1/2 cup minced mushrooms
> 3 cloves garlic, minced
> 1/3 cup toasted pine nuts, minced (optional)
> 2 tablespoons feta cheese, crumbled
> salt and pepper to taste
> 1/4 cup egg substitute
> 1 recipe Lemon Pasta (page16)

Tarragon Cream Sauce

> 3 shallots, minced
> 1 teaspoon butter
> 1/4 cup dry white wine
> 2 drops liquid smoke flavoring
> 3/4 cup lite evaporated milk mixed with 2 teaspoons
>   cornstarch
> 3 tablespoons strained nonfat yogurt (page 10)
> salt and pepper to taste

To make the ravioli filling, sauté chicken in butter until all pink is all gone. Stir in mushrooms and garlic and cook until water released from mushrooms evaporates. Stir in pine nuts, feta, salt, pepper, and egg substitute and set aside.

Make pasta and fill with the chicken mixture following instructions on page 5. Start boiling water while making sauce.

To make the sauce, cook shallots in butter until they begin to soften. Add wine, smoke flavoring, and evaporated milk mixture and cook over low heat until thickened. Mix in yogurt and season with salt and pepper.

Cook ravioli for 3 to 5 minutes, or until ravioli rise to the top. Drain and place in a warmed serving bowl. Spoon sauce over ravioli.

Each serving provides:

418	Calories	58 g	Carbohydrate
29 g	Protein	183 mg	Cholesterol
7 g	Fat	2 g	Dietary Fiber

Spinach Gnocchi with Hot Pepper Sauce

Fire-roasted red peppers come in a jar and are found in most grocery stores. They have a delicious roasted taste that gives a rich flavor to quick dishes.

Makes 6 servings

Spinach Gnocchi

> 1 pound spinach, washed, stems removed, and
>   leaves chopped
> 2 cloves garlic, minced
> 2 tablespoons chopped onion
> 1 1/2 cups lowfat ricotta cheese
> 1 teaspoon dried oregano
> 1 teaspoon dried basil
> 1 1/4 cups unbleached all-purpose flour
> pinch of nutmeg
> salt to taste
> 1 egg plus 1 egg white

Hot Pepper Sauce

> 5 shallots, minced
> 1/2 teaspoon red pepper flakes
> 1 teaspoon virgin olive oil
> 1/2 cup fire-roasted peppers, puréed
> 2 Italian plum tomatoes, peeled, seeded, and chopped
> 3/4 cup defatted chicken broth

^{1}/$_2$ cup chopped fresh parsley
^{1}/$_3$ cup dry red wine
salt and pepper to taste
dried ricotta cheese (myzithra) for garnish

To make the gnocchi, cook spinach, garlic, and onion in a pan until water from spinach evaporates. Put into a bowl and add ricotta, oregano, basil, 1 cup of the flour, nutmeg, salt, and eggs, mixing well. Work the dough with your hands adding enough of the remaining flour until you have a smooth dough. Knead well for about 5 minutes. Roll the dough into 2 long cylinders ^{1}/$_2$ inch thick. Cut into ^{3}/$_4$-inch slices. Set aside while you make the sauce.

To make the sauce, sauté the shallots and pepper flakes in the olive oil for 2 minutes. Add peppers, tomatoes, broth, parsley, and wine. Let cook, uncovered, for 30 minutes on low heat, stirring now and again. Season with salt and pepper to taste.

While sauce is cooking, boil water in a large pot and cook gnocchi for 3 minutes, or until they rise to the top. Remove from pot with a slotted spoon and place on a warm plate. Pour sauce over gnocchi. Garnish with slivers of cheese.

Each serving provides:

230	Calories	33 g	Carbohydrate
13 g	Protein	45 mg	Cholesterol
4 g	Fat	4 g	Dietary Fiber

Crab Tortellini in Shrimp Sauce

*If you can not find dried tomato flakes in your store, substitute
1 tablespoon chopped dried tomatoes.*

Makes 6 servings

Crab Tortellini

> 1 tablespoon dried tomato flakes
> 2 green onions, sliced thin
> 3 ounces mushrooms, minced
> $1/2$ pound cooked crabmeat
> $1/4$ cup freshly grated Parmesan cheese
> $1/4$ cup egg substitute
> salt and pepper to taste
> 1 pound Basic Egg Pasta (page 15)

Shrimp Sauce

> $1/2$ pound large shrimp, peeled, deveined, and chopped
> 1 garlic clove, minced
> juice of 1 lemon
> 3 tablespoons chopped sorrel
> $1/4$ cup dry white wine
> $1/3$ cup clam juice
> $1/2$ cup evaporated milk mixed with 1 tablespoon
>   cornstarch
> salt and pepper to taste
> 1 teaspoon butter (optional)
> 2 tablespoons freshly grated Parmesan cheese for garnish

To make the tortellini filling, cook tomato flakes, green onions, and mushrooms in a nonstick pan until liquid released from the mushrooms evaporates. Mix in crabmeat, Parmesan, egg substitute, and salt and pepper to taste. Set aside to cool.

Make pasta and follow the instructions for stuffing and forming tortellini on page 6.

Boil water and cook tortellini for 3 to 5 minutes, or until tortellini rise to the top. Drain.

While tortellini are cooking, put shrimp, garlic, lemon juice, sorrel, wine, and clam juice in a saucepan and cook for 5 minutes. Remove from heat and stir in evaporated milk mixture. Stir until thickened over low heat. Season with salt and pepper and stir in the butter, if desired. Spoon over tortellini. Garnish with cheese.

❖

Each serving provides:

335	Calories	40 g	Carbohydrate
27 g	Protein	224 mg	Cholesterol
6 g	Fat	2 g	Dietary Fiber

White Bean Ravioli in Dried Tomato Sauce

Combining the white beans with lamb and herbs makes a delectable ravioli.

Makes 6 servings

Ravioli

    1/2 pound lean ground lamb
    2 cloves garlic, minced
    2 teaspoons virgin olive oil
    1 1/2 cups cooked white beans
    1 teaspoon dried thyme leaves
    1 teaspoon dried basil
    1 tablespoon chopped fresh mint
    1/4 cup egg substitute
    1/2 teaspoon pepper
    1/2 teaspoon salt
    1 recipe Basic Egg Pasta (page 15)

Sauce

    1 1/2 ounces dried tomatoes
    2 1/2 cups defatted beef broth
    1 teaspoon sugar
    1/3 cup dry red wine
    2 tablespoons tomato paste
    1/4 cup chopped flat leaf parsley
    salt and pepper to taste
    freshly grated Romano cheese for garnish

To make the filling, sauté lamb and garlic in olive oil in a nonstick pan until lamb is no longer pink. Add beans, thyme, basil, mint, egg substitute, salt, and pepper and blend well.

Proceed to make ravioli according to directions on page 5.

To make the sauce, sliver tomatoes and put into a saucepan. Add broth, sugar, wine, and tomato paste. Cook, uncovered, over low heat for 20 minutes. Stir in parsley and season with salt and pepper to taste. Cook 5 minutes more.

Cook ravioli in boiling water until ravioli rise to the top of the water, about 3 minutes. Drain and place in a warmed serving bowl. Pour sauce over ravioili, sprinkle on Romano cheese, and serve.

Each serving provides:

503	Calories	67 g	Carbohydrate
27 g	Protein	208 mg	Cholesterol
13 g	Fat	5 g	Dietary Fiber

Potato Ravioli with Champagne and Caviar Sauce

The red caviar sparkles and makes this dish eye-catchingly beautiful.

Makes 8 servings

Potato Ravioli

> 1 small onion
> 2 cups mashed potatoes
> 3 to 4 tablespoons nonfat milk
> salt and pepper to taste
> 1 recipe Basic Egg Pasta (page 15) or Eggless Pasta (page 19)

Campagne and Caviar Sauce

> 3 tablespoons red caviar or more to taste
> 1 1/2 cups White Cream Sauce No. 1, substituting
> champagne for dry white wine (page 32)

Preheat oven to 325 degrees.

Leave top and bottom on onion, but remove as much of the papery skin as possible. Place in a small baking dish.Cover with foil and bake for 1 hour. Remove from oven and let cool 10 minutes. Squeeze out the onion and mash with a fork. Mix the onion with the potatoes, milk, salt, and pepper. Set aside.

Prepare ravioli as directed on page 5, filling with the potato mixture. Set aside.

In a saucepan over low heat, carefully stir the caviar into the white sauce.

Meanwhile, cook the ravioli in boiling water for 3 to 5 minutes, or until ravioli rise to the top. Drain and gently toss with the caviar sauce.

❖

Each serving provides:

316	Calories	48 g	Carbohydrate
13 g	Protein	172 mg	Cholesterol
5 g	Fat	2 g	Dietary Fiber

Artichoke Ravioli in Tomato Cream Sauce

Ravioli was the first course of Thanksgiving dinner in my husband's family. His grandmother, Molly, used to make the ravioli, then dry them on clean sheets on every bed in the house.

Makes 6 servings

Artichoke Ravioli

> 8 medium fresh artichoke bottoms
> 4 cloves garlic, minced
> 2 tablespoons minced onion
> 1/2 cup nonfat ricotta cheese
> juice of 1 lemon
> 3 tablespoons freshly grated Parmesan cheese
> 1/2 teaspoon salt
> 3/4 teaspoon white pepper
> 1/4 cup egg substitute
> 1 recipe Basic Egg Pasta (page 15), or Eggless Pasta (page 19), or Semolina Pasta (page 17)

Tomato Cream Sauce

> 1 recipe Light Tomato-Basil Sauce, substituting 3/4 cup tomato juice for the beef broth (page 28)
> 1/2 cup lite evaporated milk
> 2 tablespoons nonfat sour cream
> salt and pepper to taste
> 2 tablespoons freshly grated Parmesan, Romano, or Asiago cheese

Steam artichoke bottoms until tender. Set aside.

In a nonstick pan sprayed with vegetable spray, sauté garlic and onion until onion just begins to brown. Put mixture into a blender or food processor, add artichokes, and purée. Transfer to a bowl and add ricotta, lemon juice, Parmesan, salt, white pepper, and egg substitute and blend well. Set aside.

Make ravioli as described on page 5, filling with artichoke mixture. Lay ravioli on a tea towel sprinkled with rice flour. Fill a large pot with 3 quarts water and bring to a boil.

Meanwhile, stir evaporated milk and sour cream into tomato sauce. Warm over very low heat until just hot. Season with salt and pepper to taste.

Cook ravioli in boiling water 3 to 5 minutes, or until ravioli rise to the top. Drain and toss carefully with sauce. Sprinkle with freshly grated cheese.

Each serving provides:

383	Calories	60 g	Carbohydrate
20 g	Protein	184 mg	Cholesterol
6 g	Fat	3 g	Dietary Fiber

Sweet Potato Gnocchi

To be good, gnocchi must be light and airy. You may have to make them a couple times to get just the right consistency, but it is worth the effort.

Makes 4 servings

Sauce

> 1 cup defatted chicken broth
> 2 tablespoons minced onion
> 2 teaspoons brown sugar
> 2 tablespoons Madeira wine
> 1 cinnamon stick
> 1 teaspoon dried thyme leaves
> 1/2 cup lite evaporated milk mixed with 1 tablespoon cornstarch
> 1/2 teaspoon white pepper
> salt to taste

Gnocchi

> 2 medium sweet potatoes (about 1 cup mashed)
> 3/4 cup all-purpose unbleached flour
> pinch of salt
> pinch of nutmeg
> 1/4 cup nonfat sour cream
> 2 egg whites

To make the sauce, cook broth, onion, brown sugar, Madeira, cinnamon stick, and thyme in a small saucepan until liquid reduces by half. Remove from heat and stir in evaporated milk mixture, pepper, and salt to taste. Remove cinnamon stick and warm over low heat.

To make the gnocchi, cook sweet potatoes until tender. Peel and mash. Add flour, salt, nutmeg, sour cream, and egg whites and blend well. Knead dough for a couple minutes on a floured work surface. Add a teaspoon or more of flour, only if necessary. Dough should not be sticky, but must still feel moist and soft.

Divide dough into 6 pieces. Roll pieces into balls and roll each ball into a 1/2-inch thick cylinder. Slice each cylinder into 1-inch lengths. Cook in boiling water until gnocchi rise to the top. Drain and place on a serving platter.

Warm sauce over very low heat and pour over gnocchi.

Each serving provides:

211	Calories	41 g	Carbohydrate
9 g	Protein	1 mg	Cholesterol
1 g	Fat	2 g	Dietary Fiber

Potato and Fennel Ravioli in Green Onion Sauce

Makes about 6 servings

Potato and Fennel Ravioli

    3 large russet potatoes, peeled and diced
    1 fennel bulb, diced
    2 cloves garlic, minced
    3 to 4 tablespoons nonfat milk
    1 egg white
    salt and pepper to taste
    1 recipe Eggless Pasta (page 19)

Green Onion Sauce

    $1/2$ cup slivered green onions
    1 teaspoon virgin olive oil
    1 cup defatted chicken broth
    3 tablespoons dry sherry
    $1/4$ teaspoon white pepper
    $1/2$ cup strained nonfat yogurt (page 10)
    $1/2$ cup lite evaporated milk mixed with $1 1/2$ tablespoons
        cornstarch
    1 tablespoon freshly grated Parmesan cheese
    salt to taste

To make the filling, boil potato in water until tender. Drain and mash. Boil fennel in water until tender. Drain and purée.

Add garlic and potato to fennel and mix well. Stir in enough milk to make the potatoes the consistency of stiff mashed potatoes. Add egg white and season with salt and pepper to taste. Set aside.

Make dough for ravioli and stuff with potato filling as described on page 5.

To make the sauce, sauté green onions in olive oil for 1 minute. Add broth, sherry, and pepper. Cook for 5 minutes. Remove from heat and add yogurt, evaporated milk mixture, and cheese. Blend well and heat over very low heat until sauce thickens. Season with salt to taste.

Cook ravioli in boiling water for 4 to 5 minutes, or until ravioli rise to the top. Drain and gently toss with sauce.

Each serving provides:

383	Calories	74 g	Carbohydrate
14 g	Protein	2 mg	Cholesterol
2 g	Fat	4 g	Dietary Fiber

Turkey Ravioli with Sorrel and Thyme Sauce

When buying ground turkey, read the label to make sure it doesn't contain skin. If you are too rushed to make homemade pasta, you can use wonton wrappers for this recipe. Just follow the instructions on page 6.

Makes 8 servings

Turkey Ravioli

1 pound ground turkey
2 tablespoons finely chopped green onion
1 tablespoon finely chopped fresh thyme
1/2 cup nonfat ricotta cheese
1/2 teaspoon salt
1 teaspoon Tabasco sauce
1 egg white
1 recipe Basic Egg Pasta (page 15)

Sorrel and Thyme Sauce

3 shallots, finely chopped
1 cup dry white wine
1 teaspoon butter (optional)
4 Italian plum tomatoes, peeled and finely chopped
1 cup defatted chicken broth
1/3 cup finely chopped sorrel
2 teaspoons chopped fresh thyme
1/2 teaspoon sugar
salt and pepper to taste
freshly grated Parmesan cheese for garnish

To make the ravioli filling, put the turkey in a nonstick pan sprayed with vegetable spray and cook, breaking up the turkey as it cooks, until pink color is gone. Drain turkey and put in a bowl. Add green onion, 1 teaspoon thyme, ricotta, salt, Tabasco, and egg white and mix well. Set aside.

Make pasta dough for ravioli and fill according to the instructions on page 00. Lay ravioli on a cookie sheet sprinkled with rice flour. Start water boiling in a large pot.

To make sauce, put shallots and 1/2 cup of the wine in a saucepan. Cook until liquid reduces to 2 tablespoons. Stir in the remaining 1/2 cup wine, optional butter, tomatoes, broth, sorrel, 2 teaspoons thyme, and sugar. Cook, uncovered, over low heat for 15 minutes. Season with salt and pepper to taste and set aside.

Cook ravioli in boiling water 3 to 5 minutes, or until ravioli rise to the top. Drain and toss with sauce. Sprinkle with cheese.

Each serving provides:

321	Calories	41 g	Carbohydrate
21 g	Protein	165 mg	Cholesterol
7 g	Fat	2 g	Dietary Fiber

12

SWEET PASTA

Pasta and Lemon Timbales with Fresh Blackberry Sauce

Makes 6 servings

Timbales

> 6 ounces Lemon Pasta (page 16), cut into fettuccine
> $1/2$ cup lowfat ricotta cheese
> 4 ounces lowfat cream cheese
> $1/2$ cup sugar
> $1/2$ cup egg substitute
> pinch of fresh nutmeg
> 1 tablespoon fresh lemon zest
> 1 teaspoon vanilla

Sauce

> 2 cup fresh blackberries or 1 package frozen blackberries
> sugar to taste
> juice of 1 lemon mixed with 2 teaspoons cornstarch
> mint leaves for garnish

Make the pasta. Cook in boiling water until al dente, drain, put in cold water, and drain again.

Preheat oven 350 degrees.

To make the timbales, mix fettuccine, ricotta cheese, cream cheese, sugar, egg substitute, nutmeg, lemon zest, and vanilla until well blended.

Spray 6 custard cups with vegetable spray and sprinkle with sugar. Divide pasta mixture among cups. Put cups in a roasting pan and add water to pan to come halfway up the cups. Butter

❖

a piece of wax paper and lay it over the custard cups. Cook for 30 minutes or until firm to the touch. Remove cups from the pan and let sit 10 minutes before turning out on plates.

To make the sauce, blend berries in a food processor or blender until well crushed. Strain the juice to remove the seeds. Put juice into a saucepan and mix in sugar to taste and cornstarch mixture. Cook over low heat until mixture thickens slightly. Spoon 3 tablespoons of the sauce onto each plate and then turn out a timbale over sauce. Garnish with a mint leaf and serve.

❖

Each serving provides:

245	Calories	39 g	Carbohydrate
9 g	Protein	54 mg	Cholesterol
6 g	Fat	2 g	Dietary Fiber

Spicy Pumpkin Pasta in Whiskey Yogurt Sauce

This elegant dessert is perfect for the holidays.

Makes 6 servings

1/4 cup plus 2 tablespoons chopped pecans
1 1/2 tablespoons sugar
1 teaspoon cinnamon
1 1/2 cups nonfat milk
2 tablespoons sugar
2 tablespoons cornstarch
2 teaspoons lemon zest
2 tablespoons whiskey
1 cup lemon nonfat yogurt
1/4 cup dried cranberries
6 ounces Spicy Pumpkin Pasta, cut into fettuccine (page 22)

Put pecans, sugar, and cinnamon in a nonstick pan sprayed with butter-flavored vegetable spray and cook and shake until sugar sticks to pecans. Turn out on a piece of wax paper, separate any nuts that are sticking to each other, and cool. Set aside.

Mix milk, sugar, cornstarch, and lemon zest in a saucepan. Cook over low heat, stirring constantly, until mixture thickens (it will be quite thick). Let mixture cool slightly and then stir in whiskey, yogurt, and cranberries.

Meanwhile cook pasta in boiling water until al dente and drain. Mix pasta with yogurt sauce and divide the pasta among six plates. Sprinkle with toasted pecans.

Each serving provides:

240	Calories	39 g	Carbohydrate
7 g	Protein	2 mg	Cholesterol
6 g	Fat	2 g	Dietary Fiber

Chocolate Ravioli with Berries and Cream

Makes 8 servings

Chocolate Ravioli

> 1 1/2 cups lowfat ricotta
> 3 ounces lowfat cream cheese
> 3 tablespoons berry jam
> 1 egg, beaten
> zest of 1 lemon

1/2 recipe Chocolate Pasta (page 21)

Berries and Cream Sauce

> 3/4 cup nonfat vanilla yogurt
> 1/4 cup nonfat sour cream
> 3 to 4 tablespoons Irish whiskey
> 1 teaspoon cinnamon
> 1 1/2 cups fresh sliced strawberries, whole red raspberries, blackberries, blueberries, boysenberries or a mixture of berries
> confectioners' sugar and whole mint leaves for garnish

To make the filling, put ricotta, cream cheese, jam, egg, and lemon zest in a blender and blend until smooth. Transfer mixture to a bowl and refrigerate for 1 hour.

Make pasta dough. Roll out dough out as thinly as possible and fill as directed on page 5. Cut into 2 × 2-inch ravioli and set aside while you make the sauce.

To make the sauce, blend the yogurt, sour cream, whiskey, and cinnamon in a bowl.

Cook ravioli in boiling water until al dente and drain well. Put 3 tablespoons of the yogurt sauce on each plate and cover with 4 or 5 ravioli. Spoon on fresh berries and sprinkle with confectioners' sugar. Garnish with a whole mint leaf.

Each serving provides:

247	Calories	35 g	Carbohydrate
12 g	Protein	43 mg	Cholesterol
6 g	Fat	1 g	Dietary Fiber

Pasta with Sweet Yogurt Cheese and Fruit

Makes 6 servings

1/2 cup strained nonfat yogurt (page 10)
1/4 cup whipped cream cheese
2 tablespoons honey
1 tablespoon lemon juice
1 teaspoon vanilla
1 cup vanilla nonfat yogurt
2 tablespoons Chambord
1/2 teaspoon cardamon
12 wonton wrappers
1 tablespoon *each* cinnamon and sugar mixed together
2 cups sliced fresh fruit in season, such as bananas, kiwi,
    pineapple, strawberries, raspberries, blackberries,
    boysenberries, peaches, nectarines, grapes
sugared lemon rinds for garnish (see note)
confectioners' sugar and mint leaves for garnish

Preheat oven to 450 degrees.

In a food processor or blender, mix strained yogurt and cream cheese until well blended. Add honey, lemon juice, and vanilla. Blend until smooth. Remove to a bowl and refrigerate until ready to use. In another bowl, combine vanilla yogurt, Chambord, and cardamon. Refrigerate until ready to use.

Spray a cookie sheet with butter-flavored vegetable spray. Dip wonton wrappers in water (this removes excess starch) and drain. Lay on cookie sheet and sprinkle with cinnamon mixture. Bake 3 to 4 minutes or until golden.

To assemble dessert, spoon 1/4 cup of the vanilla yogurt mixture onto each plate. Place 1 wonton on sauced plate and then a couple of spoonfuls of the cream cheese mixture. Spoon on 1/3 cup of the fruit and top with another wonton wrapper. Sprinkle the edge of the plate with a little confectioners' sugar and garnish with a couple sugared lemon rinds and a mint leaf.

Each serving provides:

219	Calories	37 g	Carbohydrate
6 g	Protein	16 mg	Cholesterol
5 g	Fat	2 g	Dietary Fiber

Note: To make sugared lemon peels, wash lemons and remove peel in strips, getting as little of the white pith as possible. Put peels in a small saucepan and cover with water. Bring to a boil and cook 5 minutes. Remove and sprinkle with sugar. Let dry on a cookie sheet lined with wax paper.

Index

International Conversion Chart

These are not exact equivalents: they have been slightly rounded to make measuring easier.

LIQUID MEASUREMENTS

American	Imperial	Metric	Australian
2 tablespoons (1 oz.)	1 fl. oz.	30 ml	1 tablespoon
1/4 cup (2 oz.)	2 fl. oz.	60 ml	2 tablespoons
1/3 cup (3 oz.)	3 fl. oz.	80 ml	1/4 cup
1/2 cup (4 oz.)	4 fl. oz.	125 ml	1/3 cup
2/3 cup (5 oz.)	5 fl. oz.	165 ml	1/2 cup
3/4 cup (6 oz.)	6 fl. oz.	185 ml	2/3 cup
1 cup (8 oz.)	8 fl. oz.	250 ml	3/4 cup

SPOON MEASUREMENTS

American	Metric
1/4 teaspoon	1 ml
1/2 teaspoon	2 ml
1 teaspoon	5 ml
1 tablespoon	15 ml

WEIGHTS

US/UK	Metric
1 oz.	30 grams (g)
2 oz.	60 g
4 oz. (1/4 lb)	125 g
5 oz. (1/3 lb)	155 g
6 oz.	185 g
7 oz.	220 g
8 oz. (1/2 lb)	250 g
10 oz.	315 g
12 oz. (3/4 lb)	375 g
14 oz.	440 g
16 oz. (1 lb)	500 g
2 lbs	1 kg

OVEN TEMPERATURES

Farenheit	Centigrade	Gas
250	120	1/2
300	150	2
325	160	3
350	180	4
375	190	5
400	200	6
450	230	8

Also from the
GOOD-FOR-YOU
series of Cookbooks:

GOOD-FOR-YOU
SOUPS & STEWS
Cookbook